decorating
cakes&cookies

decorating
cakes & cookies
pretty cakes, clever cookies and cute cupcakes

Annie Rigg

photography by Kate Whitaker

RYLAND
PETERS
& SMALL

LONDON NEW YORK

To my darling little sister, Titch.
xx

**Design and photographic
art direction** Steve Painter
Senior editor Céline Hughes
Production controller Toby Marshall
Art director Leslie Harrington
Publishing director Alison Starling

Prop stylist Penny Markham
Indexer Hilary Bird

First published in the
United Kingdom in 2010 by
Ryland Peters & Small
20–21 Jockey's Fields
London WC1R 4BW

www.rylandpeters.com

10 9 8 7 6 5 4 3 2 1

Text © Annie Rigg 2010

Design and photographs
© Ryland Peters & Small 2010

ISBN: 978-1-84597-956-0

A CIP record for this book is available from
the British Library.

Printed and bound in China

- All spoon measurements are level, unless otherwise specified.

- Ovens should be preheated to the specified temperature. Recipes in this book were tested using a regular oven. If using a fan-assisted oven, follow the manufacturer's instructions for adjusting temperatures.

- All eggs are large, unless otherwise specified. Recipes containing raw or partially cooked egg should not be served to the very young, very old, anyone with a compromised immune system or pregnant women.

contents

cakes and cookies galore

For me, baking a batch of cookies or cupcakes is one of the most pleasurable ways to spend a morning. The magic of mixing together a few simple ingredients to create something so delicious, filling the kitchen with sweet, homey aromas is unrivalled. But sometimes you want to create something a little more special – something with an extra ounce or two of love.

Take a batch of cupcakes, add a luscious swirl of frosting and a little imagination, and you too can be a baking queen (or king). It's the little things that can make all the difference and elevate a simple tray of brownies or cookies to the next level.

You don't need any great skill or even to possess a huge array of fancy kitchen equipment to make something unique. Most of the recipes in this book use standard cake tins and equipment. All you need is a couple of piping bags, a selection of nozzles, a few assorted cookie cutters and a rainbow of food colouring pastes. All of these are now widely available in most cookshops or from online suppliers. And there are so many beautiful sprinkles and sparkles for the home baker to use that it seems crazy not to make the most of them.

Most of the recipes in this book can be made partly in advance, whether that be the cookie dough, the cake or the even the embellishments. Some of the recipes come with simple and easy-to-follow steps to guide you through the decorating techniques. There's a recipe for you however wobbly your baking skills might be, starting with simple gingerbread men (and women) right up to making sugar-paste roses for decorating a wedding cake.

These cookies, cakes and cupcakes are perfect as gifts, for that special party or just to cheer up a friend. How fabulous would it be to give your loved one a tray of Valentine's cupcakes instead of giving them an unimaginative bunch of roses or box of chocolates?

How many times have you wished you could recreate the fabulous confections you see in cake shop windows? Well, now you can. So turn the oven on, get your mixer out, go wild with the piping bag and start a love affair with sprinkles.

the basics

cake mixtures

A freestanding electric mixer makes light work of cake making, cutting down on time and energy, but you can also use an electric whisk or a good old-fashioned wooden spoon. When making cakes, it is important to remember that all ingredients, including buttermilk, soured cream and eggs, should be at room temperature before mixing.

buttermilk sponge

This base can be used for both small and large cakes. Paper cupcake cases can vary enormously in size, so it's safest to suggest filling the cases two-thirds full. This recipe makes 12–16 regular cupcakes depending on the cases used. Unfrosted cupcakes can be frozen in plastic airtight boxes.

175 g unsalted butter, softened
200 g caster sugar
2 whole eggs and 1 egg yolk, beaten
1 teaspoon vanilla extract
225 g plain flour
1 teaspoon baking powder
½ teaspoon bicarbonate of soda
125 ml buttermilk

makes 12–16 cupcakes

Cream together the butter and sugar until light and creamy. Gradually add the beaten eggs, mixing well between each addition and scraping down the side of the mixing bowl from time to time. Add the vanilla.

Sift together the flour, baking powder and bicarbonate of soda and add to the mixture in alternate batches with the buttermilk. Mix until smooth, then turn to the relevant recipe.

double choc sponge

This recipe is deep and densely chocolatey. It makes 12 regular cupcakes depending on the cases used, but can easily be doubled.

75 g dark chocolate, chopped
50 g unsalted butter, softened
175 g light brown soft sugar or light muscovado
2 eggs, beaten
½ teaspoon vanilla extract
150 g plain flour
1 rounded tablespoon cocoa powder
½ teaspoon baking powder
1 teaspoon bicarbonate of soda
a pinch of salt
125 ml soured cream
100 ml boiling water

makes about 12 cupcakes

Melt the chocolate either in a microwave or in a heatproof bowl set over a pan of barely simmering water. Cream together the butter and sugar until light and creamy. Gradually add the beaten eggs, mixing well between each addition and scraping down the side of the mixing bowl from time to time. Add the vanilla and melted chocolate and stir well. Sift the flour, cocoa, baking powder, bicarbonate of soda and salt together. Add to the mixture in alternate batches with the soured cream. Add the boiling water and mix until smooth, then turn to the relevant recipe.

plain vanilla sponge

This is a very simple, delicate sponge with a hint of vanilla. Feel free to swap the vanilla extract for finely grated unwaxed lemon zest and ½ teaspoon lemon extract.

175 g unsalted butter, softened
175 g caster sugar
3 eggs, beaten
1 teaspoon vanilla extract
175 g plain flour
3 teaspoons baking powder
3 tablespoons milk

makes 12–16 cupcakes

Cream together the butter and sugar until light and creamy. Gradually add the beaten eggs, mixing well between each addition and scraping down the side of the mixing bowl from time to time. Add the vanilla.

Sift together the flour and baking powder and add to the mixture in 2 batches. Stir in the milk. Mix until smooth, then turn to the relevant recipe.

cookie doughs

Most of the cookie recipes in this book can be made with one of the doughs below. Remember to chill the dough for a good couple of hours before rolling out and shaping into cookies. Before icing cookies, make sure they are completely cold after baking, or the icing will simply melt or slide off.

basic vanilla cookies

These biscuits will keep uniced for 3 days in an airtight box. If they've been iced, they should be eaten within 24 hours.

225 g unsalted butter, at room temperature
225 g caster sugar
1 egg, beaten
½ teaspoon vanilla extract
a pinch of salt
450 g plain flour, sifted, plus extra for dusting

Cream together the butter and sugar until light and creamy. Add the beaten egg, vanilla and salt and mix well.

Gradually add the flour and mix until incorporated. Bring together into a dough, then flatten into a disc. Wrap in clingfilm and refrigerate for 2 hours.

Roll the dough out on a lightly floured work surface to a thickness of 3–4 mm, then turn to the relevant recipe.

Remember that once you have stamped out the shapes required in the individual recipes, you can gather the remaining dough together into a ball and re-roll to make more shapes. The shapes will then need to be refrigerated for a further 15 minutes before baking.

gingerbread biscuits

These biscuits will keep uniced for 3 days in an airtight box. If they've been iced, they should be eaten within 24 hours.

375 g plain flour
½ teaspoon baking powder
1 teaspoon bicarbonate of soda
1 teaspoon ground cinnamon
3 teaspoons ground ginger
¼ teaspoon ground cloves
¼ teaspoon ground nutmeg
¼ teaspoon ground allspice
a pinch of cayenne pepper
a pinch of salt
125 g unsalted butter, softened
75 g light brown soft sugar
1 egg, beaten
50 ml clear honey
50 ml molasses or black treacle
1 tablespoon freshly squeezed lemon juice

Sift together the flour, baking powder, bicarbonate of soda, spices and salt.

Cream together the butter and sugar until light and creamy. Add the beaten egg, honey, molasses and lemon juice and mix until smooth. Add the sifted dry ingredients and mix again until smooth. Knead the dough lightly, just enough to bring it together, then wrap in clingfilm and refrigerate for 2 hours.

frostings

Everyone has their favourite frosting – mine is meringue buttercream. Whether piped into mountain-high peaks or spread with an artistic flourish, it really is the icing on the cake, so go wild with the food colouring and tint your frosting any or all the colours of the rainbow. Royal icing is perfect for icing cookies, as it can be easily coloured with food colouring pastes and piped into shapes and patterns, and it sets firm on the cookies.

marshmallow frosting

This is very simple, but you really do need a sugar thermometer to check the temperature of the meringue as it cooks, otherwise it might not be a success. This frosting should be used immediately once prepared, as it will set into a firm marshmallow once cooled.

250 g caster sugar
1 tablespoon water
4 egg whites
a pinch of salt

Put all the ingredients in a heatproof bowl set over a pan of simmering water. Whisk slowly until the sugar has dissolved and the mixture is foamy. Continue cooking until the mixture reaches at least 60°C (140°F) on a sugar thermometer.

Immediately pour the frosting into the bowl of a freestanding mixer fitted with the whisk attachment (or use an electric whisk and mixing bowl) and beat on medium speed for about 3 minutes until the meringue is stiff and glossy. Use immediately.

meringue buttercream

I love this frosting. It's lighter than basic buttercream because of the meringue element, but it does take a little more effort to make. As with the Marshmallow Frosting, you really do need a sugar thermometer to check the temperature of the meringue as it cooks. Add the butter to the meringue only when the meringue is cooled otherwise the butter will melt and curdle the frosting.

200 g caster sugar
3 egg whites
250 g unsalted butter, softened and chopped
1 teaspoon vanilla extract

Put the sugar and egg whites in a heatproof bowl set over a pan of simmering water. Whisk until it reaches at least 60°C (140°F) on a sugar thermometer. Pour into the bowl of a freestanding electric mixer fitted with the whisk attachment (or use an electric whisk and mixing bowl). Beat until the mixture has doubled in volume, cooled and will stand in stiff, glossy peaks – this will take about 3 minutes.

Gradually add the butter to the cooled meringue mix, beating constantly, until the frosting is smooth. Fold in the vanilla and use immediately.

chocolate meringue buttercream

A lighter option than the Chocolate Fudge Frosting overleaf, this is perfect for piping. Any that's left over can be stored in the fridge in an airtight box for a couple of days, but bring to room temperature and beat until smooth before using.

275 g dark chocolate, chopped
225 g caster sugar
5 egg whites
a pinch of salt
450 g unsalted butter, softened and chopped

Melt the chocolate either in a microwave or in a heatproof bowl set over a pan of barely simmering water.

Put the sugar, egg whites and salt in a heatproof bowl set over a pan of simmering water. Whisk until it reaches at least 60°C (140°F) on a sugar thermometer. Pour into the bowl of a freestanding electric mixer fitted with the whisk attachment (or use an electric whisk and mixing bowl). Beat until the meringue holds stiff, glossy peaks.

Gradually add the butter, beating between each addition. Fold in the melted chocolate, then cover until ready to use.

vanilla buttercream

This simple buttercream can be made in a variety of flavours, not just vanilla. Lemon, peppermint or pistachio extract and rosewater can easily be substituted for the vanilla.

350 g unsalted butter, softened
700 g icing sugar, sifted
a few drops of vanilla extract (optional)

Put the butter in a large bowl and, using a freestanding mixer or electric whisk, cream until really soft. Gradually add the sifted icing sugar and beat until pale and smooth. Beat in the vanilla, if using.

chocolate ganache

This is a classic topping for sophisticated cakes. Use the best-quality chocolate for this recipe.

200 g dark chocolate (at least 70% cocoa solids), chopped
75 g unsalted butter
2 tablespoons double cream

Put the chocolate, butter and double cream in a heatproof bowl set over a pan of simmering water. Stir until smooth and thoroughly combined. Set aside to cool and thicken slightly before using.

chocolate fudge frosting

This is the ultimate chocolate frosting – deep and luscious. Sweep generous swirls of it on top of vanilla or chocolate cupcakes, scatter with coloured sprinkles and you'll be the cupcake queen (or king).

350 g dark chocolate, chopped
225 g unsalted butter
225 ml milk
1 teaspoon vanilla extract
450 g icing sugar, sifted

Put the chocolate and butter in a heatproof bowl set over a pan of simmering water. Stir until smooth and thoroughly combined. Set aside to cool slightly.

In another bowl, whisk together the milk, vanilla and icing sugar until smooth. Add the cooled chocolate mixture and stir until smooth. Leave the frosting to set and thicken slightly before using.

chocolate glaze

A glossy, silky-smooth glaze for perfectly coating cakes or cookies.

300 g dark chocolate, chopped
2 tablespoons sunflower or groundnut oil

Put the chocolate and oil in a heatproof bowl set over a pan of simmering water. Stir until smooth and thoroughly combined. Set aside to cool for about 10 minutes before using.

cream cheese frosting

Carrot cake is unthinkable without this frosting. Add more or less honey according to taste, as some cream cheeses can be more salty than others. The cherry on top? A dusting of ground cinnamon. Lovely.

450 g cream cheese
2–3 rounded tablespoons clear honey

Beat the ingredients together in a mixing bowl until smooth.

mascarpone frosting

This makes an excellent alternative to the more classic Cream Cheese Frosting above and can be used for carrot or banana cakes. It's also an excellent partner for summer berry cakes, and can be used as both a filling and topping for layer cakes. Add the seeds of half a vanilla pod to take it to the next level.

150 g cream cheese
150 g mascarpone
75 g unsalted butter, softened
100 g icing sugar, sifted

Beat all the ingredients together in a mixing bowl until smooth.

royal icing

This can easily be made using shop-bought royal icing sugar – simply follow the instructions on the pack. However, if you are unable to find this type of icing sugar, here's how you make the icing from scratch.

2 egg whites
500–600 g icing sugar, sifted

Beat the egg whites until foamy using a wire whisk. Gradually add the icing sugar and whisk until the desired stiffness is reached – for piping, the icing should hold a solid ribbon trail. If you're not using it immediately, cover with clingfilm.

To make shapes, fit a piping bag with the required nozzle and fill with the royal icing. Line a baking tray with baking parchment and pipe shapes onto the paper. Set aside for at least 24 hours until set solid.

Shapes will keep for up to 1 week in an airtight container. Keep the shapes between layers of greaseproof paper.

shop-bought sugar paste, regal icing and ready-to-roll fondant

These 3 types of ready-made icings are available either in the baking aisle of most supermarkets or from sugarcraft suppliers (see page 126).

Sugar paste can be coloured using food colouring paste (see page 16) and is ideal for rolling out to make shapes like flowers. It is usually used for more decorative items that need to set solid and dry quickly. See, for example, the flowers for the Rich Chocolate Celebration Cake on page 109 and Blossom Cake on page 125.

Regal icing or ready-made royal icing is slightly softer than sugar paste and can be coloured or flavoured using food colouring pastes and flavours. It is suitable as a cake covering and for modelling flowers.

Ready-to-roll fondant icing is more often used for cake coverings and will set softer than the royal or regal icing (see Blossom Cake on page 123).

All of these icings are widely available in either white or ivory, but can also be found in a variety of colours from specialist sugarcraft suppliers.

piping nozzles and bags

If you plan on making lots of decorated cakes and cookies, it is worth considering investing in a selection of piping nozzles in varying shapes and sizes. Piping bags also come in a variety of materials and sizes. Look out for easy-to-use disposable plastic piping bags that usually come in packs of 24 and can be trimmed either to a point or to fit most piping nozzles.

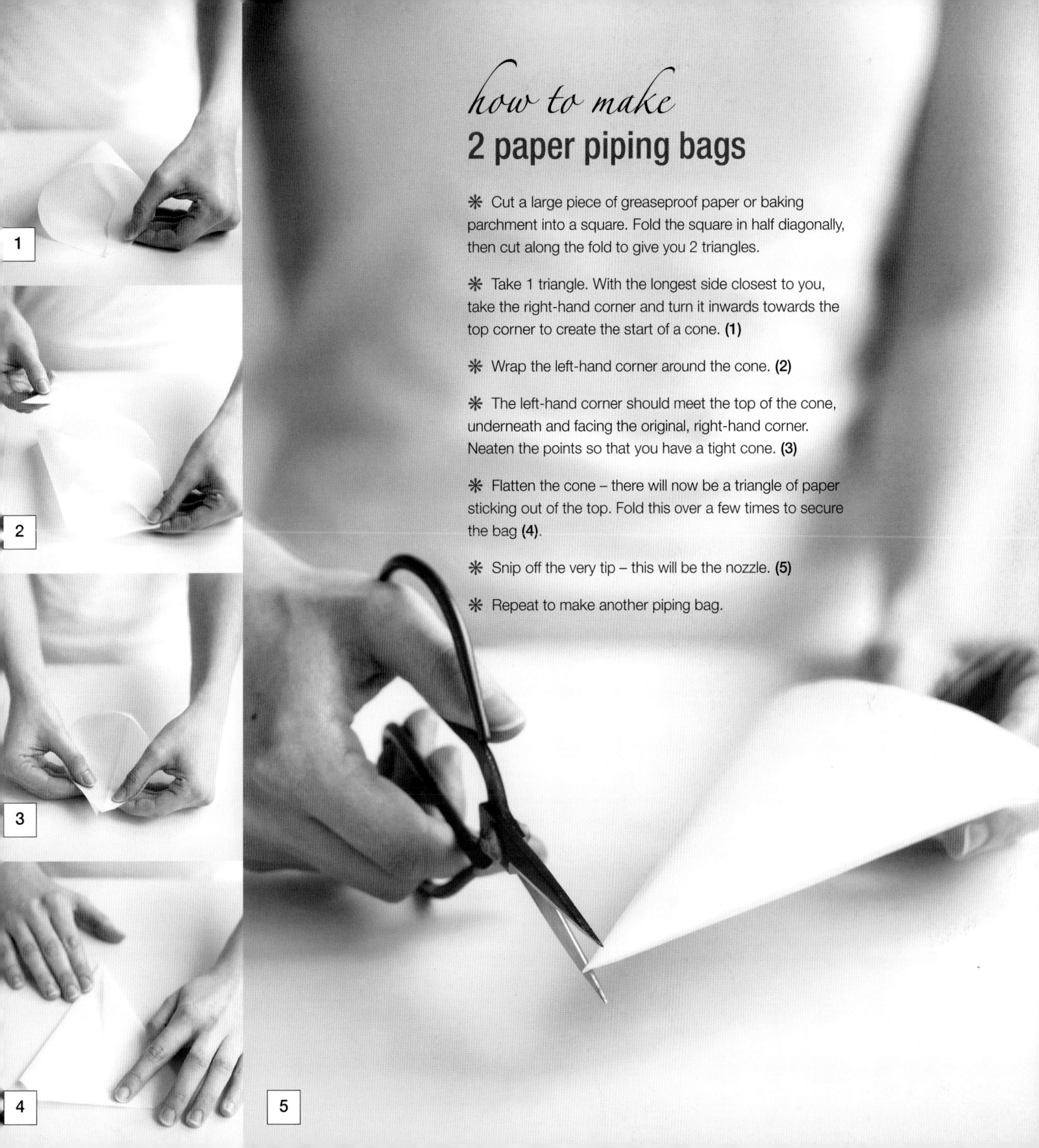

how to make
2 paper piping bags

✽ Cut a large piece of greaseproof paper or baking parchment into a square. Fold the square in half diagonally, then cut along the fold to give you 2 triangles.

✽ Take 1 triangle. With the longest side closest to you, take the right-hand corner and turn it inwards towards the top corner to create the start of a cone. **(1)**

✽ Wrap the left-hand corner around the cone. **(2)**

✽ The left-hand corner should meet the top of the cone, underneath and facing the original, right-hand corner. Neaten the points so that you have a tight cone. **(3)**

✽ Flatten the cone – there will now be a triangle of paper sticking out of the top. Fold this over a few times to secure the bag **(4)**.

✽ Snip off the very tip – this will be the nozzle. **(5)**

✽ Repeat to make another piping bag.

1

2

3

4

5

tinting royal icing

✳ Follow the recipe for Royal Icing on page 13. Using either a wooden skewer or cocktail stick, add tiny amounts of food colouring paste to the icing. (1)

✳ Mix thoroughly before adding more colouring. Remember that some colours can intensify over time, so always add the colouring in very small amounts. (2)

tinting fondant icing, sugar paste or marzipan

✳ Using a wooden skewer or cocktail stick, add tiny amounts of food colouring paste to fondant icing, sugar paste or marzipan. (3)

✳ Knead until smooth and add more colouring accordingly. Remember that some colours can intensify over time so always add the colouring gradually. (4)

food colouring pastes

These are now widely available in sugarcraft shops, good kitchen shops and online from specialist cake decorating suppliers. They come in a rainbow of colours and can be used in tiny quantities without diluting your icing, making them much easier to work with than liquid colours.

embossing sugar paste and fondant icing

Embossing tools are a very effective way of creating simple, decorative patterns on either sugar paste or fondant icing. They can be bought from cake decorating shops and sugarcraft suppliers (see page 126). Alternatively, look around your kitchen and you may find some unlikely embossing tools: the fine side of a grater gently pressed into icing can create a delicate pattern; the underside of antique silver cutlery and the points of piping nozzles can also make unusual shapes and designs.

1

2

frosting cupcakes

✳ Always make sure that any cakes you are decorating are completely cold before frosting them, otherwise the frosting will simply melt and slide off the tops.

✳ There are so many ways you can top a cupcake that there really are no rules. It's completely up to you! For simplicity, you can spread the frosting onto the top of the cakes in generous swirls using a palette knife. **(1)**

✳ If you prefer, you can pipe the frosting into more structured shapes. Fit a large piping bag with your chosen nozzle, fill the bag with frosting, twist the top of the bag so that the frosting is pushed to the end towards the nozzle and away you go! If you're not happy with your piping results, simple scoop the frosting off the top of the cake and start again.

✳ Remember that you can use different-shaped nozzles to create a variety of effects with frosting (see page 14). The Signature Cupcakes on page 92 were achieved with a star nozzle. When you've practised your piping technique and gained in confidence, try the Little Flower Pots on page 94 – they're bound to impress!

✳ There are hundreds of sprinkles to choose from for scattering over your iced cupcake. For the simplest retro decoration, cover the top of some cupcakes with frosting, spreading it right to the edges, tip your chosen sprinkles onto a plate or into a shallow bowl and simply roll the edges of the cakes into the sprinkles. **(2)**

other quick decorating ideas

✳ Look out for stencils in cake decorating shops or from sugarcraft suppliers. Made of plastic, they are available in a variety of designs and sizes. Dust either icing sugar, cocoa powder or edible coloured powders directly onto cookies or cakes.

✳ If you have patience and a steady hand, you could use a fine, soft brush to paint lustres directly onto fondant-covered cakes.

✳ Paper doilies make brilliant cheap and pretty stencils, and come in a variety of sizes and patterns. Alternatively, you could get creative with some paper and scissors and make your own stencil designs.

sprinkles

There is a huge variety of decorating sprinkles available to the home cook. They range from the simple and classic hundreds and thousands, to pastel-coloured butterflies, Valentine's hearts and miniature chocolate drops and candies. Look out for seasonal shapes in cake decorating shops or from sugarcraft suppliers.

glitters, sparkles and lustres

Use glitters, sparkles and lustres to add wow factor to your decorations. These are widely available in cake decorating shops or sugarcraft suppliers (see page 126). They come in all the colours of the rainbow and can simply be sprinkled or painted over decorations. Although edible, they should be used sparingly.

cookies

Now there's a funny thing: a cookie that wants to be a cupcake – or is it a cupcake that wants to be a cookie? The particular cookie cutter that I have used for this recipe is a cupcake topped with a candle. To make the candle more realistic I have used gold leaf for the flame, but you could simply paint the flame using food colouring pastes.

cupcake cookies

1 quantity Basic Vanilla Cookies (page 10)

1 quantity Royal Icing (page 13)

pink food colouring paste

blue food colouring paste

pink, red and white sprinkles

edible gold leaf or dust (optional)

cupcake-shaped cookie cutter

2 baking trays, lined with baking parchment

small piping bag with a fine writing nozzle, or make your own (see page 15)

mini palette knife or small knife

makes about 18

You should have rolled out the Basic Vanilla Cookie dough to a thickness of 3–4 mm on a lightly floured work surface. Using the cupcake cookie cutter, carefully stamp out shapes. Arrange them on the prepared baking trays. Gather together the off-cuts of the dough and re-roll to make more shapes. Refrigerate for 15 minutes.

Preheat the oven to 180°C (350°F) Gas 4.

Bake the cookies on the middle shelf of the preheated oven for about 12 minutes, or until golden, swapping the trays over if needed. Leave to cool on the trays for about 5 minutes before transferring to a wire rack to cool completely.

Divide the Royal Icing between 3 bowls. Tint one pink and one blue (see page 16 for help on tinting) using the food colouring pastes. Tint them the shade of pink or blue you like by very gradually adding more colouring. Leave the third bowl of icing white.

Fill the piping bag with whichever colour you want to start with. Pipe borders around the cold cookies. 'Flood' the area inside the borders with icing (see page 44 for step pictures of 'flooding'): once you have made a neat border, you can spoon icing within the borders and spread it carefully up to the edges with a mini palette knife or small knife. Leave it to dry and harden slightly before you pipe any lines on top of the flooded icing. Decorate as you like with the sprinkles.

Attach a small piece of edible gold leaf to the flame of the candle with a little brush. Leave to set before serving.

Look out for snowflake cookie cutters in sets of assorted shapes and sizes. Once covered in fondant icing, these cookies can be decorated in a vast array of nonpareils, lustres and glitters, which all help to create that festive, frosty feel.

snowflakes

1 quantity Gingerbread Biscuits (page 10)

plain flour, for dusting

icing sugar, for dusting

200–300 g white ready-to-roll fondant icing

2 tablespoons sieved apricot jam, warmed

½ quantity Royal Icing (page 13)

silver and/or white edible glitter, lustre and nonpareils

snowflake cookie cutters in assorted shapes and sizes

2 baking trays, lined with baking parchment

small piping bag with a fine writing nozzle, or make your own (see page 15)

embossing tools (optional)

festive string or narrow ribbon (optional)

makes 12—16

Preheat the oven to 180°C (350°F) Gas 4.

Take the Gingerbread Biscuit dough out of the fridge and put it on a lightly floured work surface. Roll it out to a thickness of 3–4 mm. Using the snowflake cookie cutters, carefully stamp out shapes. Arrange them on the prepared baking trays. Gather together the off-cuts of the dough and re-roll to make more shapes. If you are making these cookies to hang as Christmas decorations, using a wooden skewer, make a hole in the top of each snowflake big enough to push your ribbon through.

Bake the cookies on the middle shelf of the preheated oven for 10–12 minutes, or until firm and the edges are just starting to brown, swapping the trays over if needed. Leave to cool on the trays for about 5 minutes before transferring to a wire rack to cool completely.

Lightly dust a work surface with icing sugar. Roll out the fondant icing to a thickness of no more than 3 mm. Using the snowflake cookie cutters again, stamp out snowflakes to match each of your cookies. Lightly brush the top of each cold cookie with the warmed apricot jam. Carefully position one fondant snowflake on top of each cookie, gently smoothing into place with your hands.

Fill the piping bag with the Royal Icing and pipe a border around the edge of the fondant icing on each cookie. Decorate with lines and dots – whatever takes your fancy. While the royal icing is still wet, sprinkle edible glitter, lustres and nonpareils over it so that they stick in place.

Using embossing tools (see page 17), press decorative patterns into the fondant icing, if you like. If you have made holes in the cookies to hang them, you will need to push the skewer into the fondant to make a hole in the same place. Leave the cookies to dry, then push a length of string or ribbon through each hole and tie a knot to secure.

These little biscuits work best when made into simple shapes such as stars and flowers. The decoration is in the colourful 'stained-glass' centre, so the simpler the shape of the biscuit, the more eye-catching the design. These are a great idea for children's parties – kids love the pretty colours and jewel-like effect.

stained-glass biscuits

1 quantity Basic Vanilla Cookies (page 10)

1 bag fruit-flavoured boiled sweets

selection of shaped cookie cutters

2 baking trays, lined with baking parchment

makes about 24

You should have rolled out the Basic Vanilla Cookie dough to a thickness of 3–4 mm on a lightly floured work surface. Using the cookie cutters, carefully stamp out shapes. Arrange them on the prepared baking trays. Using smaller cutters, cut out a shape in the centre of each biscuit. Gather together the off-cuts of the dough and re-roll to make more shapes. Refrigerate for 15 minutes.

Preheat the oven to 180°C (350°F) Gas 4.

Divide the boiled sweets into separate colours and pop into plastic food bags. Using a rolling pin or pestle and mortar, crush the sweets into small pieces.

Take the trays of biscuits out of the fridge. Carefully fill the empty space in the centre of each biscuit with the crushed sweets in an even, thin layer and no thicker than the depth of the biscuits.

Bake one tray at a time on the middle shelf of the preheated oven for about 12 minutes, or until the biscuits are pale golden and the sweets have melted to fill the space.

Leave the biscuits to cool on the trays until the 'stained glass' has set.

Look out for images of Russian dolls and use them as templates for these cookies. I found a shape I liked and photocopied it in 3 different sizes. Simply cut out the paper template, lay it onto the rolled-out cookie dough and cut around it using a small, sharp knife. You can also now find cookie-cutter kits to make your own shapes.

russian dolls

1 quantity Basic Vanilla Cookies or Gingerbread Biscuits (page 10)

plain flour, for dusting

2 quantities Royal Icing (page 13)

red food colouring paste

black food colouring paste

red, pink and white heart- and star-shaped sugar sprinkles

russian doll-shaped paper templates

2 baking trays, lined with baking parchment

small piping bag with a fine writing nozzle, or make your own (see page 15)

mini palette knife or small knife

makes about 8—10 depending on size

If you haven't already done so, roll out the Basic Vanilla Cookie or Gingerbread Biscuit dough to a thickness of 3–4 mm on a lightly floured work surface. Lay your paper templates directly on top of the dough and cut around using a small, sharp knife. Arrange them on the prepared baking trays. Gather together the off-cuts of the dough and re-roll to make more shapes. Refrigerate for 15 minutes.

Preheat the oven to 180°C (350°F) Gas 4.

Bake the cookies on the middle shelf of the preheated oven for about 12 minutes, or until firm, swapping the trays over if needed. Leave to cool on the trays for about 10 minutes before transferring to a wire rack to cool completely.

Divide the Royal Icing between 3 bowls. Tint one red and one black (see page 16 for help on tinting) using the food colouring pastes. Leave the third bowl of icing white.

Fill the piping bag with whichever colour you want to start with. Pipe borders around the cold cookies. If you want to make the 'belly' of the doll in the other colour of icing, you will need to create a border for this too. 'Flood' the area inside the borders with icing (see page 44 for step pictures of 'flooding'): once you have made a neat border, you can spoon icing within the borders and spread it carefully up to the edges with a mini palette knife or small knife. Leave to dry and harden slightly before going any further.

Pipe in the rest of the design and the dolls' faces. Now the fun starts: you can feather the icing using a wooden skewer or cocktail stick (see pages 48–9 for steps on feathering) or pipe small flowers, dots, squiggles and whatever you like over the dolls. Arrange the shaped sugar sprinkles all over. Leave to set before serving.

This recipe makes approximately 12 cookies or 6 pairs of shoes, depending on the size of your cutters. Why not decorate the cookies to match your favourite outfit or to coordinate with a special occasion such as a hen night or wedding?

a girl can never have enough shoes

1 quantity Basic Vanilla Cookies or Gingerbread Biscuits (page 10)

plain flour, for dusting

200–300 g white ready-to-roll fondant icing or sugar paste

red food colouring paste

icing sugar, for dusting

2 tablespoons sieved apricot jam, warmed

pearly nonpareils

edible sugar diamonds (optional)

high-heeled shoe-shaped cookie cutter

2 baking trays, lined with baking parchment

very small, round cookie cutter

embossing tools

makes about 6 pairs

If you haven't already done so, roll out the Basic Vanilla Cookie or Gingerbread Biscuit dough to a thickness of 3–4 mm on a lightly floured work surface. Using the shoe cookie cutter, carefully stamp out shapes. Arrange them on the prepared baking trays. Gather together the off-cuts of the dough and re-roll to make more shapes. Refrigerate for 15 minutes.

Preheat the oven to 180°C (350°F) Gas 4.

Bake the cookies on the middle shelf of the preheated oven for about 12 minutes, or until firm, swapping the trays over if needed. Leave to cool on the trays for about 5 minutes before transferring to a wire rack to cool completely.

Divide the fondant icing (or sugar paste) into 2. Tint one portion red (see page 16 for help on tinting) using the food colouring paste. Tint it the shade of red you like by very gradually adding more colouring. Leave the other half white.

Lightly dust a work surface with icing sugar. Roll out the 2 colours of fondant icing to a thickness of no more than 2 mm. Using the shoe cookie cutter again, stamp out shoes to match each of your cookies. Using the very small, round cookie cutter, stamp out circles all over each shoe. Carefully remove the circles and reserve them.

Lightly brush the top of each cold cookie with the warmed apricot jam. Carefully position one fondant shoe on top of each cookie, gently smoothing into place with your hands. Use any off-cuts to make bows, ribbons and embellishments for your shoes. Take your little red reserved circles and slot them into the holes in your white shoes. Repeat with the white circles and red shoes. Stick the embellishments onto the shoes with a tiny dab of cold water.

Using embossing tools (see page 17), decorate the shoes with patterns and gently press pearly nonpareils and/or sugar diamonds into the designs. Leave to set before serving.

Gingerbread people come in a variety of shapes, sizes and states of undress! You could make simple gingerbread men (or women) with their more traditional decoration of currant eyes and buttons, or go for something a little more unique such as Adam and Eve, complete with fondant-icing fig leaves protecting their modesty. To make the leaves, you can either attempt to cut out the shapes freehand using a small, sharp knife, or you can make a paper template, lay it on the icing and cut around it. The flower in Eve's hair is made like those on page 125.

gingerbread adam and eve

1 quantity Gingerbread Biscuits (page 10)

plain flour, for dusting

100 g white ready-to-roll fondant icing

green food colouring paste

icing sugar, for dusting

gingerbread man-shaped cookie cutter

2 baking trays, lined with baking parchment

very small and medium flower-shaped cutters

makes about 8—10 depending on size

Preheat the oven to 180°C (350°F) Gas 4.

Take the Gingerbread Biscuit dough out of the fridge and put it on a lightly floured work surface. Roll it out to a thickness of 3–4 mm. Using the gingerbread man cookie cutter, carefully stamp out shapes. Arrange them on the prepared baking trays. Gather together the off-cuts of the dough and re-roll to make more shapes.

Bake the biscuits on the middle shelf of the preheated oven for 10–12 minutes, or until firm and the edges are just starting to brown, swapping the trays over if needed. Leave to cool on the trays for about 5 minutes before transferring to a wire rack to cool completely.

If you'd like to make the white flowers as hair accessories for Eve, divide the fondant icing into 2. (If you are only making fig leaves, you don't need to divide it up.) Tint one portion green (see page 16 for help on tinting) using the food colouring paste. Tint it the shade of green you like by very gradually adding more colouring. Leave the other half white.

Lightly dust a work surface with icing sugar. Roll out the 2 colours of fondant icing to a thickness of no more than 2 mm. Cut out fig leaf shapes with a small, sharp knife or use a paper template. Mark out the leaf veins with a cocktail stick or the back of a knife. Stamp out flowers with the very small flower-shaped cookie cutter for Eve's extra covering. To make flowers for Eve's hair, use the medium flower-shaped cutter and follow the instructions on page 125.

Stick the fig leaves, bikini flowers and hair accessories onto each cold biscuit in the correct position with a little dab of cold water!

Look out for sets of assorted Easter-related cookie cutters, but if you can't find them, make paper templates, lay over the cookie dough and carefully cut out using a small, sharp knife. I've made my Easter bunnies using an extra-large cutter, but feel free to use a smaller breed!

easter eggs and bunnies

1 quantity Basic Vanilla Cookies or Gingerbread Biscuits (page 10)

plain flour, for dusting

2 quantities Royal Icing (page 13)

brown food colouring paste

pink food colouring paste

blue food colouring paste

lilac food colouring paste

black food colouring paste

white nonpareils or sugar strands

easter egg-shaped cookie cutters

bunny rabbit-shaped cookie cutter

2 baking trays, lined with baking parchment

small piping bag with a fine writing nozzle, or make your own (see page 15)

mini palette knife or small knife

narrow gingham ribbon (optional)

makes about 10—12 depending on size

If you haven't already done so, roll out the Basic Vanilla Cookie or Gingerbread Biscuit dough to a thickness of 3–4 mm on a lightly floured work surface. Using the cookie cutters, carefully stamp out egg and bunny shapes. Arrange them on the prepared baking trays. Gather together the off-cuts of the dough and re-roll to make more shapes. Refrigerate for 15 minutes.

Preheat the oven to 180°C (350°F) Gas 4.

Bake the biscuits on the middle shelf of the preheated oven for about 12 minutes, or until firm, swapping the trays over if needed. Leave to cool on the trays for about 5 minutes before transferring to a wire rack to cool completely.

Divide the Royal Icing between 6 bowls. Tint each one a different colour (see page 16 for help on tinting) using the food colouring pastes. You will only need a tiny amount of the black icing. Leave the last bowl of icing white.

Fill the piping bag with whichever colour you want to start with. Pipe borders around the cold egg-shaped biscuits. 'Flood' the area inside the borders with icing (see page 44 for step pictures of 'flooding'): once you have made a neat border, you can spoon icing within the borders and spread it carefully up to the edges with a mini palette knife or small knife. Leave to dry and harden slightly before going any further.

Pipe in the rest of the design: draw lines, squiggles and dots over each egg. Set aside to dry completely.

Repeat the same technique for icing the bunnies using brown icing. Pipe in noses, mouths and eyes with the black icing. Finish off each rabbit with a fluffy tail: pipe a large blob of white icing in the correct position and scatter with the nonpareils or sugar strands.

Once the icing has completely set, tie a length of gingham ribbon around the neck of each bunny and serve alongside the eggs.

These cookies are like a ray of sunshine on a grey day. Any type of flower-shaped cookie cutter can be used. Why not use a variety of shapes and sizes to make a flower cookie bouquet?

sunflowers

1 quantity Basic Vanilla Cookies (page 10)

200–300 g white ready-to-roll fondant icing

yellow food colouring paste

½ quantity Royal Icing (page 13)

black food colouring paste

icing sugar, for dusting

1 tablespoon sieved apricot jam, warmed

10–12-cm sunflower-shaped cookie cutter

2 baking trays, lined with baking parchment

small piping bag with a small star-shaped nozzle

makes about 12 depending on size

You should have rolled out the Basic Vanilla Cookie dough to a thickness of 3–4 mm on a lightly floured work surface. Using the sunflower cookie cutter, carefully stamp out shapes. Arrange them on the prepared baking trays. Gather together the off-cuts of the dough and re-roll to make more shapes. Refrigerate for 15 minutes.

Preheat the oven to 180°C (350°F) Gas 4.

Bake the biscuits on the middle shelf of the preheated oven for about 12 minutes, or until golden, swapping the trays over if needed. Leave to cool on the trays for 5 minutes before transferring to a wire rack to cool completely.

Tint the fondant icing yellow (see page 16 for help on tinting) using the yellow food colouring paste and the Royal Icing black using the black food colouring paste.

Now see opposite for instructions on how to decorate the biscuits.

how to decorate
sunflowers

✳ Lightly dust a work surface with icing sugar. Roll out the yellow fondant icing to a thickness of no more than 2 mm.

✳ Using the sunflower cookie cutter again, stamp out flowers to match each of your biscuits. Lightly brush the top of each cold biscuit with the warmed apricot jam. Carefully position one fondant flower on top of each biscuit, gently smoothing into place with your hands. You might find it easier to transfer the fondant flower while it's still in the cutter. **(1)**

✳ Fill the piping bag with the black royal icing and pipe rosettes into the middle of each sunflower. **(2)**

✳ Leave to set before serving.

Watch out! Here's an invasion of edible bugs and critters that children will love to help decorate. Let them loose with the piping bag and food colouring (within reason!), and leave them to design their own critters.

garden critters

1 quantity Basic Vanilla Cookies (page 10)

1 quantity Royal Icing (page 13)

food colouring pastes in assorted colours

critter-shaped cookie cutters (e.g. snail, ladybird, butterfly, caterpillar)

2 baking trays, lined with baking parchment

small piping bag with a fine writing nozzle, or make your own (see page 15)

mini palette knife or small knife

makes about 12—18 depending on size

You should have rolled out the Basic Vanilla Cookie dough to a thickness of 3–4 mm on a lightly floured work surface. Using the critter cookie cutters, carefully stamp out shapes. Arrange them on the prepared baking trays. Gather together the off-cuts of the dough and re-roll to make more shapes. Refrigerate for 15 minutes.

Preheat the oven to 180°C (350°F) Gas 4.

Bake the biscuits on the middle shelf of the preheated oven for about 12 minutes, or until golden, swapping the trays over if needed. Leave to cool on the trays for about 5 minutes before transferring to a wire rack to cool completely.

Divide the Royal Icing between the number of bowls you need for your colours of icing. Tint each one a different colour (see page 16 for help on tinting) using the food colouring pastes.

Fill the piping bag with whichever colour you want to start with. Pipe borders around the cold biscuits. 'Flood' the area inside the borders with icing (see page 44 for step pictures of 'flooding'): once you have made a neat border, you can spoon icing within the borders and spread it carefully up to the edges with a mini palette knife or small knife.

Leave it to dry and harden slightly before you pipe any lines or other features on top of the flooded icing. Leave to set before serving.

This simple shortbread can be adapted into a variety of flavours and colours. Match the colour of the sugar to the flavour of the cookies: yellow for lemon, green for pistachio and purple for lavender. Decide on one flavour and corresponding colour scheme before you start.

225 g unsalted butter, softened

125 g caster sugar

1 egg, beaten

1 teaspoon vanilla extract

300 g plain flour, plus extra for dusting

a pinch of salt

4 tablespoons granulated sugar

yellow, red, green and/or purple food colouring pastes to match your colour scheme

1 tablespoon milk

one flavouring of your choice

2 tablespoons finely chopped mixed peel or 125 g chopped glacé cherries or 125 g chopped pistachios or 2 tablespoons dried lavender flowers, to match your colour scheme

2 baking trays, lined with baking parchment

makes about 20

sugared refrigerator cookies

Cream together the butter and caster sugar until light and creamy in the bowl of a freestanding mixer (or use an electric whisk and mixing bowl). Add the egg and vanilla and mix well. Sift the flour and salt into the mixture, along with the flavouring you have chosen, and mix again until smooth and the flour is incorporated.

Tip the dough onto a very lightly floured work surface and divide into 2. Roll each piece of dough into a sausage shape roughly 5–6 cm in diameter, wrap tightly in greaseproof paper and refrigerate until solid – at least 2 hours.

Preheat the oven to 150°C (300°F) Gas 3.

Tip the granulated sugar into a plastic food bag. Using the tip of a wooden skewer, gradually add the colour of food colouring paste you have chosen to match the flavour of the cookie, mixing well until the desired shade is reached. Tip the coloured sugar onto a baking tray. Remove the cookie dough logs from the fridge and brush them with the milk. Roll in the coloured sugar to coat evenly.

Using a sharp knife, cut the logs into 5-mm slices and arrange on the prepared baking trays. Bake on the middle shelf of the preheated oven for about 15 minutes, or until pale golden. Leave to cool on the trays for 5 minutes before transferring to a wire rack to cool completely.

1   **2**   **3**

These cookies make beautiful wedding favours. They are best made from simple shapes: squares, rounds or hearts all work well. Ice the cookies in colours to match the wedding colour scheme and design. Why not personalize them for each guest and use as place settings?

monogrammed wedding cookies

1 quantity Basic Vanilla Cookies
(page 10)

1 quantity Royal Icing (page 13)

blue food colouring paste (or
whichever colour you need for
your colour scheme)

*square, round and/or heart-
shaped cookie cutters*

*2 baking trays, lined with baking
parchment*

*small piping bag with a fine
writing nozzle, or make your
own (see page 15)*

mini palette knife or small knife

*makes about 12—18
depending on size*

You should have rolled out the Basic Vanilla Cookie dough to a thickness of
3–4 mm on a lightly floured work surface. Using the cookie cutters, carefully stamp
out shapes. Arrange them on the prepared baking trays. Gather together the off-cuts
of the dough and re-roll to make more shapes. Refrigerate for 15 minutes.

Preheat the oven to 180°C (350°F) Gas 4.

Bake the cookies on the middle shelf of the preheated oven for about 12 minutes,
or until golden, swapping the trays over if needed. Leave to cool on the trays for
about 5 minutes before transferring to a wire rack to cool completely.

Divide the Royal Icing between 2 bowls. Tint one blue (see page 16 for help on
tinting) using the food colouring paste. Leave the second bowl of icing white.

Fill the piping bag with whichever colour you want to start with. Pipe borders around
the cold cookies. **(1)** Once you have made a neat border, you can spoon icing within
the borders and spread it carefully up to the edges with a mini palette knife or small
knife. This is called 'flooding'. **(2)** Leave it to dry and harden slightly.

Now fill your clean piping bag with the other colour of icing. Pipe lines, dots or other
simple decorations on the cookies, then your chosen monogram in the centre. **(3)**
Leave to set before serving.

These elegant cookies are a snip to make and wouldn't look out of place at the smartest tea table. The dough can be prepared in advance and the cookies baked off the day before you plan to decorate them. The feathering technique is useful to know because it can be used for royal icing as well as this chocolate glaze. Feel free to be as expressive as you like with the flourishes. I have made these cookies in different-sized rounds, but they could easily be stamped out into hearts or squares.

black and white cookies

175 g plain flour, plus extra for dusting

50 g cocoa powder

½ teaspoon baking powder

½ teaspoon bicarbonate of soda

a pinch of salt

125 g unsalted butter, softened

225 g caster sugar

1 egg, beaten

1 teaspoon vanilla extract

to decorate

100 g white chocolate, chopped

1 quantity Chocolate Glaze (page 12)

5-cm and 7-cm round cookie cutters

2 baking trays, lined with baking parchment

small piping bag with a fine writing nozzle, or make your own (see page 15)

mini palette knife or small knife

makes about 16

Sift together the flour, cocoa powder, baking powder, bicarbonate of soda and salt into a mixing bowl.

Cream together the butter and sugar until light and creamy in the bowl of a freestanding mixer (or use an electric whisk and mixing bowl). Add the beaten egg and vanilla and mix well. Add the sifted dry ingredients and mix again until smooth. Bring together into a dough and knead very lightly and briefly. Flatten into a disc, wrap in clingfilm and refrigerate for a couple of hours until very firm.

When you are ready to start baking, preheat the oven to 180°C (350°F) Gas 4.

Dust the work surface with flour and roll out the chilled cookie dough to a thickness of about 3 mm. Using the cookie cutters, carefully stamp out rounds. Arrange them on the prepared baking trays. Gather together the off-cuts of the dough and re-roll to make more rounds.

Bake on the middle shelf of the preheated oven for 12–15 minutes, or until crisp. Leave to cool on the trays for a couple of minutes before transferring to a wire rack to cool completely.

To decorate the cookies, put the white chocolate in a heatproof bowl set over a pan of barely simmering water. Stir until smooth and thoroughly melted. Put the cookies back on some baking parchment to catch any drips while you are decorating them.

Fill your piping bag with the molten white chocolate and get a wooden skewer or cocktail stick ready for the feathering.

Now see overleaf for instructions on how to decorate the cookies.

how to decorate
black and white cookies

✳ Pour some of the Chocolate Glaze over each cookie with a spoon **(1)**.

✳ Spread the glaze neatly over the cookie, just to the edge, with the back of the spoon or with a mini palette knife. Repeat with the remaining cookies **(2)**.

✳ Working quickly, pipe dots of white chocolate over the dark chocolate glaze on just a few of the cookies **(3)**.

✳ Using the point of a wooden skewer or cocktail stick, drag the white chocolate into the chocolate glaze to create a feathered effect. Repeat with the remaining cookies and leave to set before serving **(4)**.

These elegant and sophisticated cookies look like they belong in a chic Parisian pâtisserie, but are actually incredibly easy to make. They can be tinted almost any colour imaginable and filled with jam, cream, buttercream or ganache.

macaroons

150 g icing sugar

75 g ground almonds

3 egg whites

a pinch of salt

a pinch of cream of tartar

50 g caster sugar

pink food colouring paste

green food colouring paste

yellow food colouring paste

1 tablespoon cocoa powder

1 quantity Vanilla Buttercream (page 12 – vanilla or flavoured with lemon, pistachio, etc. to suit your colour scheme), Chocolate Ganache (page 12), whipped double cream or jam

4 small piping bags with 1-cm plain nozzles

2 baking trays, lined with baking parchment

makes about 20

Preheat the oven to 170°C (325°F) Gas 3.

Sift the icing sugar and ground almonds together into a bowl.

Put the egg whites in the bowl of a freestanding electric mixer fitted with the whisk attachment (or use an electric whisk and mixing bowl). Add the salt and cream of tartar and whisk until the egg whites form soft peaks. Add the caster sugar a teaspoon at a time, whisking well between each addition. Continue whisking until the mixture is stiff and glossy.

Fold the icing sugar and ground almonds into the mixture using a large metal spoon. Divide the mixture between 4 bowls and tint 3 of them a different colour using the food colouring pastes and a wooden skewer or cocktail stick. Fold in gently until evenly dyed. Stir the cocoa powder into the fourth bowl.

Fill each piping bag with a different colour of macaroon mixture. Pipe 5-cm discs onto the prepared baking trays. Sharply tap the tray on the work surface – this will knock any extra air bubbles out of the macaroons. Set aside for 10 minutes to allow the mixture to settle before baking.

Bake on the middle shelf of the preheated oven for 8–9 minutes. Leave to cool on the trays for 5 minutes before transferring to a wire rack to cool completely.

Sandwich the macaroons together with your choice of buttercream, Chocolate Ganache, whipped cream or jam and serve immediately.

This is the kind of treat to put a smile on your face – it has something to do with the nostalgic combination of chocolate, peppermint and hundreds and thousands. You could also try dipping just the top cookie in chocolate glaze and coating in sprinkles too.

mint chocolate kisses

175 g dark chocolate, chopped

175 g unsalted butter

2 medium eggs

225 g light muscovado sugar

250 g self-raising flour

¾ teaspoon baking powder

a pinch of salt

minty buttercream

75 g unsalted butter, softened

150 g icing sugar, sifted

½–1 teaspoon peppermint extract

to decorate

200 g dark chocolate, chopped

hundreds and thousands

2 baking trays, lined with baking parchment

makes about 18

Put the chocolate and butter in a heatproof bowl set over a pan of barely simmering water. Stir until smooth and thoroughly combined.

Put the eggs and sugar in the bowl of a freestanding electric mixer fitted with the whisk attachment (or use an electric whisk and mixing bowl) and beat until pale and light. Add the chocolate mixture and mix until smooth.

Sift together the flour, baking powder and salt. Add to the mixing bowl and stir until smooth. Bring together into a dough, cover and refrigerate for a couple of hours.

When you are ready to start baking, preheat the oven to 180°C (350°F) Gas 4.

Remove the cookie dough from the fridge and pull off walnut-sized pieces. Roll into balls and arrange on the prepared baking trays. Bake in batches on the middle shelf of the preheated oven for about 12 minutes, or until the cookies are crisp on the edges but slightly soft in the middle. Leave to cool on the trays for a few minutes before transferring to a wire rack to cool completely.

To make the minty buttercream, put the butter in a large bowl and, using a freestanding mixer or electric whisk, cream until really soft. Gradually add the sifted icing sugar and beat until pale and smooth. Add peppermint extract to taste.

Sandwich the cold cookies together with the minty buttercream.

To decorate, put the chocolate in a heatproof bowl set over a pan of barely simmering water. Stir until smooth and melted. Leave to cool slightly. Half-dip the cookies in the melted chocolate, sprinkle with hundreds and thousands and leave on baking parchment to set before serving.

small cakes

I would love someone forever if they were to make a tray of these for me! Paper cupcake cases come in hundreds of colours and designs, and the choice available for Valentine's cupcakes is vast – look out for polka dots, love hearts and foil cases in shiny red and pink. Red velvet cake is not just for Valentine's, but made in miniature and topped with sparkly red marzipan hearts, it's a marriage made in cupcake heaven.

red velvet valentine's cupcakes

225 g plain flour

1 teaspoon bicarbonate of soda

2 rounded tablespoons cocoa powder

a pinch of salt

225 g unsalted butter, softened

225 g caster sugar

2 eggs, beaten

1 teaspoon vanilla extract

225 ml buttermilk, at room temperature

1 teaspoon red food colouring paste (ruby or Christmas red is best)

1 quantity Marshmallow Frosting (page 11)

marzipan hearts

200 g natural marzipan

red food colouring paste (ruby or Christmas red is best)

edible red glitter

1–2 muffin tins, lined with paper cupcake cases

makes 18

Preheat the oven to 180°C (350°F) Gas 4.

Sift together the flour, bicarbonate of soda, cocoa powder and salt in a mixing bowl.

Cream together the butter and sugar until light and creamy in the bowl of a freestanding mixer (or use an electric whisk and mixing bowl). Gradually add the beaten eggs, mixing well between each addition and scraping down the side of the mixing bowl from time to time. Add the vanilla.

With the mixer on low speed, add the sifted dry ingredients to the mixture, alternating with the buttermilk. Mix until smooth, then add the red food colouring paste – you will need to add enough to make the mixture deep red and the quantity needed may vary depending on the brand and colour used. Stir until evenly mixed.

Divide the mixture between the paper cupcake cases, filling them two-thirds full, and bake on the middle shelf of the preheated oven for 20 minutes, or until well risen and a skewer inserted into the middle of the cupcakes comes out clean. Leave to cool in the tins for 5 minutes before transferring to a wire rack to cool completely.

Spoon the Marshmallow Frosting on top of the cold cupcakes, swirling and shaping it with the back of a spoon to get a lovely peaked effect.

Now see overleaf for instructions on how to make the marzipan hearts.

1

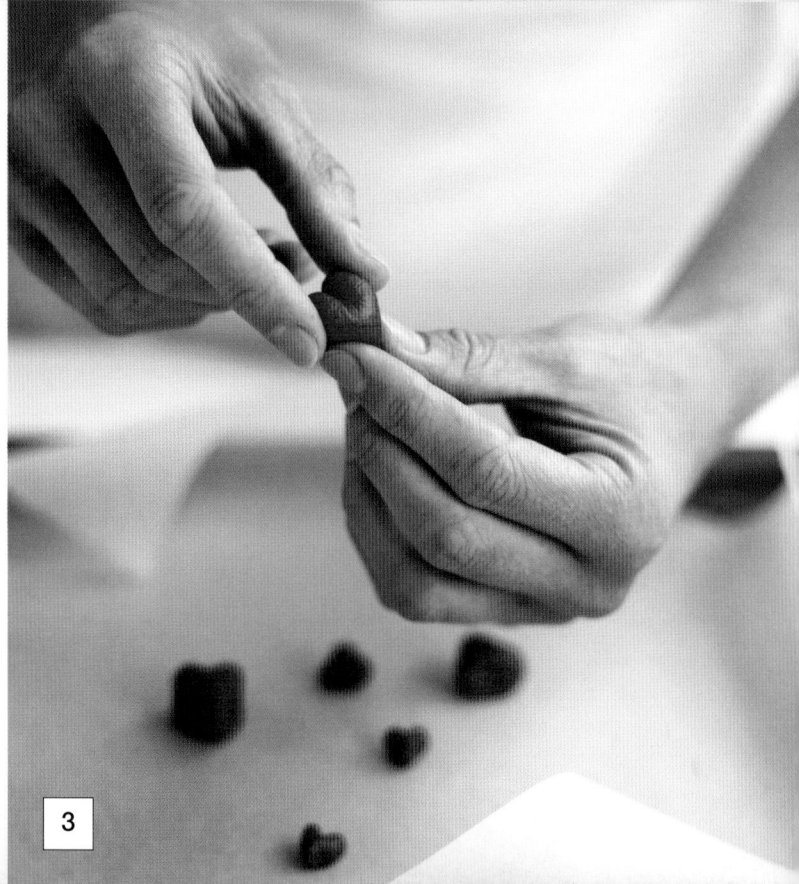

2

how to make
marzipan hearts

✳ Tint the marzipan red (see page 16 for help on tinting) using the food colouring paste.

✳ Make one heart at a time. Break off a small piece of marzipan and roll into a cylinder in the palm of your hand. **(1)**

✳ Gently squeeze the ends towards each other to make the top of the heart. **(2)**

✳ Using your fingers, squeeze the other end into a point to make the bottom of the heart. **(3)**

✳ Put on baking parchment and repeat to make more hearts in assorted sizes. Dust with edible red glitter. **(4)**

✳ Sit the hearts on top of the frosted cupcakes just before serving.

3

These delicately spiced little cakes are topped with maple syrup-flavoured cream cheese frosting and then adorned with a wafer-thin slice of candied pear and a cluster of caramelized nuts. The candied pears can be made in advance and stored on baking parchment in a cool, dry place until ready to serve.

autumn spiced honey cakes

175 g unsalted butter, softened

100 g light muscovado sugar

75 g clear honey

3 eggs, beaten

175 g plain flour

3 teaspoons baking powder

2 teaspoons ground ginger

1 teaspoon ground cinnamon

a pinch of ground allspice

a pinch of salt

finely grated zest of ½ orange

finely grated zest of ½ unwaxed lemon

2 tablespoons freshly squeezed orange juice

Cream Cheese Frosting (page 13 and made with maple syrup instead of clear honey)

candied nuts

150 g caster sugar

100 g mixed shelled nuts, lightly toasted

pear wafers

50 g caster sugar

freshly squeezed juice of ½ lemon

3 firm pears, e.g. conference

1–2 muffin tins, lined with paper cupcake cases

1 baking tray, oiled

1–2 baking trays, lined with baking parchment

makes 12

Preheat the oven to 180°C (350°F) Gas 4.

Cream together the butter, sugar and honey until light and creamy in the bowl of a freestanding mixer (or use an electric whisk and mixing bowl). Gradually add the beaten eggs, mixing well between each addition and scraping down the side of the mixing bowl from time to time.

Sift together the flour, baking powder, spices and salt. Add to the cake mixture and mix until thoroughly combined. Add the grated orange and lemon zest and orange juice and mix again.

Divide the mixture between the paper cupcake cases, filling them two-thirds full, and bake on the middle shelf of the preheated oven for 20–25 minutes, or until well risen and a skewer inserted into the middle of the cupcakes comes out clean. Leave to cool in the tins for 5 minutes before transferring to a wire rack to cool completely.

To make the candied nuts, put the sugar and 3 tablespoons water in a saucepan over low/medium heat. Leave until the sugar has completely dissolved, then raise the heat and bring the syrup to a steady boil. Continue to cook without stirring until the syrup turns a deep amber colour. Working quickly, tip the toasted nuts into the syrup and stir to coat. Using 2 spoons, divide the candied nuts into 12 piles (one for each cupcake) on the oiled baking tray. Leave to cool and harden.

To make the pear wafers, preheat the oven to 110°C (225°F) Gas ¼.

Put the sugar, 100 ml water and lemon juice in a small saucepan and bring to the boil. Simmer for 2 minutes, then remove from the heat and leave to cool. Slice the pears no thicker than 3 mm – this is easiest using a mandoline. Dip each slice into the syrup and shake off any excess. Lay the pears in a single layer on the lined baking trays and bake on the middle and lower shelves of the oven for about 2 hours, or until beginning to crisp up and turn golden. Turn the slices over on the parchment and, if using 2, swap the trays over halfway through cooking. Leave to cool – they will crisp up further as they cool.

When the cupcakes, candied nuts and pear wafers are all cold, spread the Cream Cheese Frosting over the cupcakes and decorate with a pile of candied nuts and a single pear wafer.

Here's an idea for the child in all of us! You can really go to town with the decorating and pick any animal that has distinctive enough features to represent in sprinkles, sweets and coloured icing. I've made a rabbit, monkey, teddy bear and pig, but the choice is yours.

animal-face cupcakes

1 quantity Buttermilk Sponge (page 9)

1 quantity Meringue Buttercream (page 11)

to decorate

food colouring pastes in assorted colours

75 g dark chocolate, chopped

marshmallows in assorted sizes and colours

jelly beans in assorted colours

liquorice strips

white, milk and dark chocolate buttons in assorted sizes

chocolate vermicelli and other sprinkles

white sugar strands or nonpareils

a little Royal Icing (page 13)

1–2 muffin tins, lined with paper cupcake cases

small piping bag with a fine writing nozzle, or make your own (see page 15)

makes 12—16

Preheat the oven to 180°C (350°F) Gas 4.

Divide the Buttermilk Sponge mixture between the paper cupcake cases, filling them two-thirds full, and bake on the middle shelf of the preheated oven for 20 minutes, or until well risen and a skewer inserted into the middle of the cupcakes comes out clean. Leave to cool in the tins for 5 minutes before transferring to a wire rack to cool completely.

How you decorate these cupakes depends on the animals you have chosen. These are just tips for making facial features.

Tint the Meringue Buttercream into as many different colours as you need by dividing it between separate bowls and tinting each one using food colouring pastes (see page 16 for help on tinting).

To make a teddy bear, monkey or any other brown animal face, put the chocolate in a heatproof bowl set over a pan of barely simmering water. Stir until smooth and melted. Add to one bowl of meringue buttercream and stir until well mixed.

Cover the tops of the cold cupcakes in your tinted buttercream, spreading smoothly with a palette knife.

Use marshmallows in assorted sizes to make noses and snouts. Cover with tinted buttercream to match the rest of the face and push into the face to attach. You can also cut a large marshmallow in half and pinch or squash with your fingers to shape into ears. Stick at the top of the cupcake.

Use halved jelly beans for nostrils or large eyes. Strips of liquorice positioned under the nose make good mouths or whiskers.

Use white, milk and dark chocolate buttons, individually or stacked, for ears. Stick in place with a dab of buttercream.

Chocolate vermicelli and other sprinkles and nonpareils make ideal fur, while sugar strands can be used for buck teeth.

Complete the features with thinly piped black Royal Icing to make little eyes and dainty smiles or just to glue features in place.

The crystallized flowers on these delicate cupcakes are truly stunning and very easy to make. They do need at least 12 hours to dry properly, but once you've made them they will keep for up to 4 days in a cool, dry place. I have used 4–5 spring flowers per cake, but you could use fewer (and of different varieties) if you prefer.

spring flower cupcakes

1 quantity Buttermilk Sponge (page 9)

1 quantity Meringue Buttercream (page 11)

pink food colouring paste

yellow food colouring paste

lilac food colouring paste

crystallized flowers

fresh primroses

fresh violets and violas

1 egg white

125 g caster sugar

1–2 muffin tins, lined with paper cupcake cases

makes 12—16

Make the crystallized flowers the day before you plan to serve these cupcakes. See overleaf for instructions on how to make the crystallized flowers.

Preheat the oven to 180°C (350°F) Gas 4.

Divide the Buttermilk Sponge mixture between the paper cupcake cases, filling them two-thirds full, and bake on the middle shelf of the preheated oven for 20 minutes, or until well risen and a skewer inserted into the middle of the cupcakes comes out clean. Leave to cool in the tins for 5 minutes before transferring to a wire rack to cool completely.

Divide the Meringue Buttercream between 3 bowls and tint each one a different colour (see page 16 for help on tinting) using the food colouring pastes. Tint them the shade you like by very gradually adding more colouring.

Spread the buttercream over the cold cupcakes and arrange the crystallized flowers on top.

how to crystallize
flowers and petals

✳ This is a very simple and beautiful way to decorate cakes. Make sure that the flowers you choose are not poisonous, are unsprayed and are clean and dry.

✳ If you are using whole flowers like primroses, violets and violas, snip the flowers off the stems, leaving just a small bit of the stem.

✳ If you are using rose petals, carefully pull the petals off the flower heads.

✳ Very lightly beat 1 egg white with a fork until it is only just foamy (this will only take about 5 seconds). Put a few tablespoons of caster sugar in a bowl.

✳ Crystallize one petal (or flower) at a time. Use a pastry brush to lightly coat both sides of the petal with the egg white. **(1)**

✳ Sprinkle the wet petal with caster sugar all over (both sides) until evenly coated in sugar. **(2)**

✳ Arrange the petals in a single layer on a wire rack lined with baking parchment and leave to dry for at least 1 hour, but preferably up to 12 hours. The petals shouldn't touch while they are drying. **(3)**

✳ Flowers and petals will keep for up to 4 days, but are best used on the day they are ready as the natural colour will fade over time.

✳ As well as flowers and petals, you can also crystallize strands of red-, white- and blackcurrants. Follow the same method as for the flowers above.

100 g dark chocolate, chopped

175 g plain flour

50 g cocoa powder

3 rounded teaspoons
baking powder

a pinch of salt

200 g unsalted butter, softened

200 g light muscovado sugar

4 eggs, beaten

1 teaspoon vanilla extract

4 rounded tablespoons soured
cream, at room temperature

to decorate

4 tablespoons sieved apricot
jam, warmed

chocolate truffles

1 quantity Chocolate Ganache
(page 12)

shop-bought crystallized violets
and roses, edible gold and
silver leaf, chocolate-coated
coffee beans, chopped
pistachio nuts and/or melted
white chocolate (or your choice
of edible decorations)

*20 x 30-cm baking tin, greased
and lined with baking
parchment*

*small square, round and
triangular cookie cutters*

makes 16–20

This neat idea looks tricky, but in reality it's easy peasy. Why not serve this box of chocolates after a smart dinner – it's dessert and petits fours all rolled into one.

box of chocolates

Preheat the oven to 180°C (350°F) Gas 4.

Put the chocolate in a heatproof bowl set over a pan of barely simmering water. Stir until smooth and thoroughly melted.

Sift together the flour, cocoa powder, baking powder and salt.

Cream together the butter and sugar until light and creamy in the bowl of a freestanding mixer (or use an electric whisk and mixing bowl). Gradually add the beaten eggs, mixing well between each addition and scraping down the side of the mixing bowl from time to time. Add the vanilla and melted chocolate.

With the mixer on low speed, add the sifted dry ingredients to the mixture, alternating with the soured cream.

Pour the mixture into the prepared baking tin, spread level and bake on the middle shelf of the preheated oven for 20–25 minutes, or until a skewer inserted into the middle of the cake comes out clean. Leave to cool in the tin for 10 minutes before transferring to a wire rack to cool completely.

Refer to the step instructions on the page opposite for decorating the chocolates.

how to decorate
the chocolates

✳ Stamp out shapes from the cold cake using the shaped cookie cutters. (1)

✳ Brush the tops and sides with the warmed apricot jam and set the little cakes on a wire rack.

✳ You can pop a chocolate truffle on top of some of the little cakes to make a bump.

✳ Spoon the Chocolate Ganache over the cakes, spreading it evenly with a palette knife and letting it drip down. (2)

✳ Leave to set for 20 minutes, then decorate with the toppings, such as crystallized violets and roses, edible gold or silver leaf, chocolate-coated coffee beans, chopped pistachio nuts and melted white chocolate drizzled over with a piping bag. (3)

These cupcakes have hidden jewels in the mixture – nuggets of almonds, dried cranberries and white chocolate chips – and they are topped with a snowdrift of meringue frosting. Make the sugar-paste snowflakes a couple of days before serving and leave to dry before decorating with royal icing and assorted sprinkles and glitter.

snowflake cupcakes

50 g blanched almonds, chopped

175 g plain flour

3 teaspoons baking powder

a pinch of salt

175 g unsalted butter, softened

175 g caster sugar

3 eggs, beaten

2 teaspoons vanilla extract

3 tablespoons soured cream or milk, at room temperature

100 g white chocolate chips

75 g dried cranberries

white nonpareils

1 quantity Marshmallow Frosting (page 11)

edible glitter and lustre in silver and white

snowflakes

icing sugar, for dusting

250 g white sugar paste

½ quantity Royal Icing (page 13)

small snowflake-shaped cutter

1–2 muffin tins, lined with paper cupcake cases

small piping bag with a fine writing nozzle, or make your own (see page 15)

makes 12—16

Make the snowflakes the day before you make the cupcakes. Lightly dust a clean, dry work surface with icing sugar. Roll the sugar paste out to a thickness of no more than 3 mm. Using the snowflake cutter, stamp out the desired number of shapes. Set aside on baking parchment to dry out overnight.

The next day, fill the piping bag with the Royal Icing and pipe little dots onto the sugar-paste snowflakes. Sprinkle with edible glitter and/or lustre and leave to set.

When you are ready to bake the cupcakes, preheat the oven to 180°C (350°F) Gas 4.

Put the almonds on a baking tray and toast in the preheated oven for 5–7 minutes, or until just turning golden. Remove from the oven and leave to cool.

Sift together the flour, baking powder and salt.

Cream together the butter and sugar until light and creamy in the bowl of a freestanding mixer (or use an electric whisk and mixing bowl). Gradually add the beaten eggs, mixing well between each addition and scraping down the side of the mixing bowl from time to time. Add the vanilla.

Add the sifted dry ingredients to the mixture and mix until just incorporated. Stir in the soured cream. Fold in the almonds, chocolate chips and cranberries.

Divide the mixture between the paper cupcake cases, filling them two-thirds full, and bake on the middle shelf of the preheated oven for 20–25 minutes, or until well risen and a skewer inserted into the middle of the cupcakes comes out clean. Leave to cool in the tins for 5 minutes before transferring to a wire rack to cool completely.

Tip the white nonpareils into a bowl or saucer. Frost the cupcakes with the Marshmallow Frosting and decorate the edges with the nonpareils, using the instructions on page 18. Scatter some edible glitter and/or lustre over the top and finish off each cupcake with a sugar-paste snowflake.

Who doesn't love carrot cake? This light, moist recipe is made more delicious with the addition of coconut and marmalade. The marzipan carrots and rabbits can be made days in advance and will keep well in an airtight box. However, be sure to place them on top of the cakes just before serving, otherwise the food colouring will bleed into the frosting.

carrot cake cupcakes

175 g plain flour

1 teaspoon baking powder

½ teaspoon bicarbonate of soda

½ teaspoon ground cinnamon, plus extra for dusting

2 eggs

200 g light brown soft sugar

175 ml groundnut oil

1 teaspooon vanilla extract

2 tablespoons fine-cut marmalade

50 g shelled walnuts or pecans, toasted

175 g grated carrots

50 g desiccated coconut

1 egg white

1 quantity Cream Cheese Frosting (page 13)

carrots and rabbits

300 g natural marzipan

orange food colouring paste

brown food colouring paste

white mini-marshmallows

white sugar strands

angelica

1–2 muffin tins, lined with paper cupcake cases

makes 16—18

Start making the marzipan carrots the day before you make the cupcakes. Tint two-thirds of the marzipan orange using the orange food colouring paste (see page 16 for help on tinting). Tint it the shade of orange you like by very gradually adding more colouring. Break off small nuggets of the marzipan and roll between your hands to make carrot shapes. Using the blunt end of a wooden skewer, push a small hole into the top of each carrot.

Use the remaining marzipan to make the rabbits. Tint it brown using the brown food colouring paste. Break off small nuggets of marzipan and roll between your hands for the rabbits' bodies, and do the same with smaller pieces for the heads. Carefully press a head onto a body. Make tiny ears from the marzipan and carefully attach to the top of each rabbit head. Dip the tip of a wooden skewer into the brown food colouring paste and paint eyes, a nose and a mouth onto each rabbit. Attach a mini-marshmallow for a fluffy tail and use the white sugar strands to make the rabbits' teeth. Now leave the rabbits and carrots to dry out overnight on a sheet of baking parchment in an airtight box.

The next day, cut the angelica into very fine matchsticks about 1–2 cm long and push into the small hole in the top of each carrot. When you are ready to make the cupcakes, preheat the oven to 180°C (350°F) Gas 4.

Sift together the flour, baking powder, bicarbonate of soda and cinnamon. In another bowl, whisk together the whole eggs, sugar, oil, vanilla and marmalade. Add the nuts, grated carrots and coconut and mix again.

Add the sifted dry ingredients and mix lightly. Put the egg white in a grease-free bowl and whisk until it forms stiff peaks, then gently fold into the mixture.

Divide the mixture between the paper cupcake cases, filling them three-quarters full, and bake in the preheated oven for 25 minutes, or until well risen and a skewer inserted into the middle of the cupcakes comes out clean. Leave to cool in the tins for 5 minutes before transferring to a wire rack to cool completely.

Spread the Cream Cheese Frosting over the cold cupcakes, dust with cinnamon and arrange the marzipan carrots and rabbits on top.

This is an edible festive wreath to take centre stage for a Christmas afternoon tea. Make the cupcakes in silver and gold cases in an assortment of sizes. The white and dark chocolate leaves can be made in advance and kept in a cool, dry place until required.

christmas wreath

1 quantity Buttermilk Sponge (page 9)

1 quantity Meringue Buttercream (page 11)

red sugar-coated candies

edible gold and silver glitter

chocolate leaves

200 g white chocolate, chopped

200 g dark chocolate, chopped

fresh bay leaves

muffin tin, lined with 8–10 silver or gold paper cupcake cases

mini-muffin tin, lined with 8–10 silver or gold paper cases in the coordinating size

makes 1 large wreath

Preheat the oven to 180°C (350°F) Gas 4.

Divide the Buttermilk Sponge mixture between the paper cases, filling them two-thirds full, and bake on the middle shelf of the preheated oven for 12–25 minutes. The time will vary according to the size of the cakes – keep an eye on them and take them out when they are well risen and a skewer inserted into the middle of the cakes comes out clean. Leave to cool in the tins for 5 minutes before transferring to a wire rack to cool completely.

While the cakes are cooling, make the chocolate leaves. You will need about 40 leaves, so these can be done in batches. Refer to the step instructions overleaf for making the chocolate leaves.

Spread the Meringue Buttercream over the cold cakes and arrange the cakes in a wreath shape on a large serving platter. Decorate each cake with the white and dark chocolate leaves. Scatter over the red candies to look like berries and dust with edible gold and silver glitter.

melting chocolate

Weigh out the required amount of chocolate and chop into small pieces. Put it in a clean, dry heatproof bowl and sit over a pan of barely simmering water. Do not allow the bottom of the bowl to touch the water. Once the chocolate is half melted, you can remove the pan from the heat and allow the chocolate to melt slowly. Stir until smooth before using.

how to make
chocolate leaves

✳ Wash and thoroughly dry the bay leaves.

✳ Melt the white and dark chocolate separately as described on the opposite page.

✳ Using a clean, dry pastry brush, spread a thin, even layer of melted chocolate over one side of the bay leaves. Leave to set. **(1)**

✳ Repeat with a second layer of chocolate.

✳ Once all the chocolate has set, very carefully peel off the leaves. **(2)** Repeat as necessary to make enough leaves.

✳ You can make chocolate leaves from other fresh, firm leaves, but make sure they are not poisonous.

✳ You can also make simple shapes such as stars using melted chocolate. Melt the chocolate as described on the page opposite, fill a small piping bag with it and pipe star shapes onto baking parchment. Leave to set until firm, then carefully peel off and use to decorate cupcakes.

✳ See also page 121 for instructions on making chocolate sheets to cut into panels and other shapes.

Each of these little cakes is topped with meringue buttercream and a selection of candies and sprinkles in all the colours of the rainbow. If you had a very large serving dish you could arrange the cupcakes in a rainbow shape. They're perfect for a children's party – you could even get the children to decorate their own at the party.

a rainbow of cupcakes

1 quantity Buttermilk Sponge (page 9)

1 quantity Meringue Buttercream (page 11)

food colouring pastes in all colours, e.g. red, orange, yellow, green, blue, indigo and violet

little sweets in colours to match your food colouring pastes

1–2 muffin tins, lined with paper cupcake cases

makes 12—16

Preheat the oven to 180°C (350°F) Gas 4.

Divide the Buttermilk Sponge mixture between the paper cupcake cases, filling them two-thirds full, and bake on the middle shelf of the preheated oven for 20 minutes, or until well risen and a skewer inserted into the middle of the cupcakes comes out clean. Leave to cool in the tins for 5 minutes before transferring to a wire rack to cool completely.

Divide the Meringue Buttercream between 7 bowls (or however many you need for the colours you're using) and tint each one a different colour (see page 16 for help on tinting) using the food colouring pastes. Tint them the shade you like by very gradually adding more colouring.

Spread the buttercream over the cold cupcakes and arrange the coordinating sweets on top.

A step up from the more traditional butterfly fairy cakes you used to make with your mum when you were little, these have painted sugar-paste wings to make them look ready for flight! Once you have mastered the technique for making and painting the wings, you can let your imagination run wild with colours and patterns.

butterfly cupcakes

1 quantity Buttermilk Sponge (page 9)

1 quantity Meringue Buttercream (page 11)

hundreds and thousands

butterflies

icing sugar, for dusting

250 g white sugar paste

1 quantity Royal Icing (page 13)

pink food colouring paste

yellow food colouring paste

brown food colouring paste

1–2 muffin tins, lined with paper cupcake cases

butterfly-shaped cutter

small piping bag with a fine writing nozzle, or make your own (see page 15)

mini palette knife or small knife

makes 12—16

Preheat the oven to 180°C (350°F) Gas 4.

Divide the Buttermilk Sponge mixture between the paper cupcake cases, filling them two-thirds full, and bake on the middle shelf of the preheated oven for 20 minutes, or until well risen and a skewer inserted into the middle of the cupcakes comes out clean. Leave to cool in the tins for 5 minutes before transferring to a wire rack to cool completely.

Spread the Meringue Buttercream over the cold cupcakes and scatter the hundreds and thousands over them.

Get your butterfly cutter, piping bag and a wooden skewer or cocktail stick ready.

Refer to the step instructions overleaf for making the sugar-paste butterflies.

When the butterflies are completely dry, place matching pairs of wings on the cupcakes, pushing them at an angle into the topping.

how to make
sugar-paste butterflies

✳ Lightly dust a clean, dry work surface with icing sugar. Roll the sugar paste out to a thickness of no more than 3 mm.

✳ Using the butterfly-shaped cutter, stamp out the desired number of shapes. **(1)**

✳ Cut each butterfly in half through the body to create 2 wings and set aside on baking parchment to dry out overnight. **(2)**

✳ Divide the Royal Icing between 3 bowls. Tint one pink and one yellow (see page 16 for help on tinting) using the food colouring pastes. Tint them the shade of pink or yellow you like by very gradually adding more colouring. Leave the third bowl of icing white.

✳ Pour 2–3 tablespoons of the white icing into your piping bag.

✳ Working on one wing at a time, pipe a border around the wing. 'Flood' the inner half of the wing, nearest the butterfly's body, with white icing (see page 44 for step pictures of 'flooding') by spreading it to the inner edge with the mini palette knife or small knife.

✳ Fill the other half of the wing with either pink or yellow icing, spreading to the outer edge and inwards to meet the white icing. **(3)**

✳ Using the tip of the skewer, drag the coloured icing into the white to create a feathered effect. **(4)** Leave to dry. Repeat with the remaining wings.

✳ Tint a small amount of the white icing brown and use to pipe a small line down the middle of each wing to create the body. **(5)**

✳ Leave the wings to dry completely.

Topped with a cascade of summer berries and a swirl of strawberry-scented, delicate pink buttercream, these cupcakes are the height of summer sophistication. You could also top the cakes with just one type of fruit if you prefer. Check out the suppliers on page 126 for the prettiest paper cases to complete the picture.

summer berry cupcakes

1 quantity Buttermilk Sponge (page 9)

1 quantity Meringue Buttercream (page 11)

3–4 tablespoons sieved strawberry jam

assorted summer berries, e.g. strawberries, raspberries, blueberries and redcurrants

icing sugar, for dusting

1–2 muffin tins, lined with paper cupcake cases

makes 12–16

Preheat the oven to 180°C (350°F) Gas 4.

Divide the Buttermilk Sponge mixture between the paper cupcake cases, filling them two-thirds full, and bake on the middle shelf of the preheated oven for 20 minutes, or until well risen and a skewer inserted into the middle of the cupcakes comes out clean. Leave to cool in the tins for 5 minutes before transferring to a wire rack to cool completely.

Put the Meringue Buttercream in a bowl and fold in the strawberry jam. Spread the frosting over the cold cupcakes and arrange the summer berries on top of each one in a lovely cascade. Dust with icing sugar.

These little carved pumpkin-shaped cakes each have their own spooky grin. The selection of Halloween cake sprinkles and paper cupcake cases available in specialist cake decorating shops and online is vast. Look out for orange, green or black paper cases and orange sanding sugar and nonpareils to scatter over the tops and on the serving dish.

jack-o'-lanterns

1 quantity Buttermilk Sponge (page 9)

1 quantity Meringue Buttercream (page 11)

black food colouring paste

orange food colouring paste

orange sanding sugar or nonpareils

green jelly beans or fruity pastilles, for the stalks

Halloween sugar sprinkles (optional), to decorate the serving dish

1–2 muffin tins, lined with orange paper cupcake cases

small piping bag with a small star-shaped nozzle

makes 12—16

Preheat the oven to 180°C (350°F) Gas 4.

Divide the Buttermilk Sponge mixture between the paper cupcake cases, filling them two-thirds full, and bake on the middle shelf of the preheated oven for 20 minutes, or until well risen and a skewer inserted into the middle of the cupcakes comes out clean. Leave to cool in the tins for 5 minutes before transferring to a wire rack to cool completely.

Put the Meringue Buttercream in a bowl. Take out 6 tablespoons and put in a separate bowl. Tint this quantity black (see page 16 for help on tinting) using the black food colouring paste. Colour the remaining, large bowl of buttercream orange using the orange food colouring paste.

Spread the orange buttercream over the cold cupcakes, spreading evenly with a palette knife. Using the blunt end of a knife or a wooden skewer, make indents in the buttercream to resemble ridges in the pumpkins. Scatter orange sanding sugar or nonpareils over the buttercream until evenly coated.

Fill the piping bag with the black buttercream. Pipe eyes, a nose and a mouth onto the orange frosting to make jack-o'-lantern faces. Lay the cupcakes on their side and stick one green jelly bean into the top of each cupcake to make the stalks.

Scatter the serving dish with Halloween sugar sprinkles, if using, and arrange the cupcakes on top to serve.

Whoever would have thought that lurking under these bobble hats are cupcakes? These penguins take a little more time to frost than some other recipes, but the cupcakes, hats, beaks and wings can all be made in advance. Scatter crushed-up meringues over the serving dish to complete the snowy, polar theme.

fat penguins in bobble hats

1 quantity Buttermilk Sponge (page 9)

1 quantity Vanilla Buttercream (page 12)

black food colouring paste

tiny white chocolate drops

125 g white ready-to-roll fondant icing

yellow food colouring paste

red food colouring paste

ready-made meringues (optional), to decorate the serving dish

icing sugar, for dusting

muffin tin, lined with 8–10 paper cupcake cases

mini-muffin tin, lined with 8–10 paper cases in the coordinating size

makes 8—10

Preheat the oven to 180°C (350°F) Gas 4.

Divide the Buttermilk Sponge mixture between the paper cases, filling them two-thirds full, and bake on the middle shelf of the preheated oven for 12–25 minutes. The time will vary according to the size of the cakes – keep an eye on them and take them out when they are well risen and a skewer inserted into the middle of the cakes comes out clean. Leave to cool in the tins for 5 minutes before transferring to a wire rack to cool completely.

Put two-thirds of the Vanilla Buttercream in a bowl and tint it black (see page 16 for help on tinting) using the black food colouring paste. Leave the rest of the buttercream white.

To make the penguins, remove the paper cases from all the cold cakes and trim the top off each cake to make it level. Lay the larger cupcakes upside down on the clean work surface and dab a little of the buttercream on the top. Lay a mini-muffin upside down on top of each larger cupcake. Using a palette knife, spread black buttercream smoothly all over the penguins, leaving the area for the tummy unfrosted. Spread white buttercream into the tummy area. Press 2 tiny white chocolate drops onto each penguin's face for the eyes. Using a cocktail stick, dab a little black food colouring onto the middle of each eye.

To make the wings, hats and beaks, take 25 g of the fondant icing and tint it yellow using the food colouring paste. Break off small nuggets of the icing and shape into triangles for the beaks. Stick one onto the front of each penguin. To make the wings, colour half of the remaining icing black using the food colouring paste. Pinch off hazelnut-sized pieces and shape and flatten into wings. Press one wing onto either side of each penguin. Use the remaining icing to make the bobble hats. Tint three-quarters of it red and leave the remainder white. Roll and pinch the red icing into cone shapes and push the ends so that they droop. Roll the white icing into small balls and prick each one all over with a cocktail stick to make it look like a pompom. Stick one to the end of each hat. Carefully place a hat on top of each penguin.

Crush the meringues and scatter over a serving dish, lif you like. Dust with icing sugar. Position the penguins around the snow scene.

These wintery chaps have a certain twinkle about them – each one seems to have a slightly different expression. Scatter extra desiccated coconut on the serving dish to make a snowy landscape. The marzipan carrots, eyes and mouths can be made in advance and stored in an airtight box until ready to use.

snowmen in scarves

75 g natural marzipan

orange food colouring paste

black food colouring paste

1 quantity Buttermilk Sponge (page 9)

1 quantity Marshmallow Frosting (page 11)

500 g desiccated coconut

16–20 red candy-coated chocolate drops

liquorice sticks, cut into 8–10 x 1-cm lengths

8–10 large chocolate buttons

muffin tin, lined with 8–10 paper or silver cupcake cases

mini-muffin tin, lined with 8–10 paper or silver cases in the coordinating size

8–10 cocktail sticks

narrow festive ribbon, cut into 8–10 x 25-cm lengths

Start making the marzipan noses, mouths and eyes the day before you make the snowmen. Tint three-quarters of the marzipan orange using the orange food colouring paste (see page 16 for help on tinting). Tint it the shade of orange you like by very gradually adding more colouring. Break off small nuggets of the marzipan and roll between your hands to make carrot shapes.

Tint the remaining marzipan black using the black food colouring paste and roll into tiny balls, allowing roughly 4 for each snowman's mouth and 1 for each eye. Make the balls for the eyes slightly larger than the ones for the mouth. Now leave everything to dry out overnight on a sheet of baking parchment in an airtight box.

The next day, when you are ready to make the snowmen, preheat the oven to 180°C (350°F) Gas 4.

Divide the Buttermilk Sponge mixture between the paper cases, filling them two-thirds full, and bake on the middle shelf of the preheated oven for 12–25 minutes. The time will vary according to the size of the cakes – keep an eye on them and take them out when they are well risen and a skewer inserted into the middle of the cakes comes out clean. Leave to cool in the tins for 5 minutes before transferring to a wire rack to cool completely.

Using a palette knife, spread the Marshmallow Frosting smoothly over the tops of the cold cakes, right to the edges. Before the frosting sets, coat the top of each cake with desiccated coconut. Press the marzipan noses into the middle of each smaller cake and arrange the tiny black marzipan balls as the eyes and mouths. Press the candy-coated chocolate drops down the middle of each larger cupcake to make buttons. To make the hats, dab a tiny amount of frosting in the middle of each chocolate button and stick the liquorice onto it.

Lay each large cupcake on its side with the coconut facing you and the buttons in a vertical line. Carefully push a cocktail stick into what is now the top of each cake so that there is still 2 cm of the stick exposed. Push a mini-muffin onto the cocktail stick to make the head. Tie a length of ribbon around the neck of each snowman and balance the hat on top of his head.

Scatter desiccated coconut over a serving dish and position the snowmen on it.

These cupcakes would be perfect for a wedding or sophisticated hen party. The letters are made from royal icing and should be finished at least 48 hours before serving to allow them time to harden. They will keep for up to a week, so you can make them well in advance. They can also be tinted using food colouring pastes according to your colour scheme, or sprinkled with glitter, as we've done here.

signature cupcakes

1 quantity Royal Icing (page 13)

edible glitter in a colour of your choice

1 quantity Buttermilk Sponge (page 9)

1 quantity Marshmallow Frosting (page 11)

small piping bag with a small star-shaped nozzle

baking tray, lined with baking parchment

1–2 muffin tins, lined with silver paper cupcake cases

small piping bag with a large star-shaped nozzle

makes 12—16

Start making the royal-icing letters 2 days before you make the cupcakes. Make sure the Royal Icing is stiff-peak consistency – i.e. stiff enough to hold its shape once piped – so add more icing sugar if you need to.

See opposite for instructions on how to make the letters.

When you are ready to make the cupcakes, preheat the oven to 180°C (350°F) Gas 4.

Divide the Buttermilk Sponge mixture between the paper cupcake cases, filling them two-thirds full, and bake on the middle shelf of the preheated oven for 20 minutes, or until well risen and a skewer inserted into the middle of the cupcakes comes out clean. Leave to cool in the tins for 5 minutes before transferring to a wire rack to cool completely.

Fill the piping bag with the large star-shaped nozzle with the Marshmallow Frosting. Pipe generous swirls over each cold cupcake and sprinkle with edible glitter. Leave to set for about 30 minutes.

Very carefully peel the set royal-icing letters off the baking parchment and arrange on top of each cupcake, pushing them gently into the frosting.

1

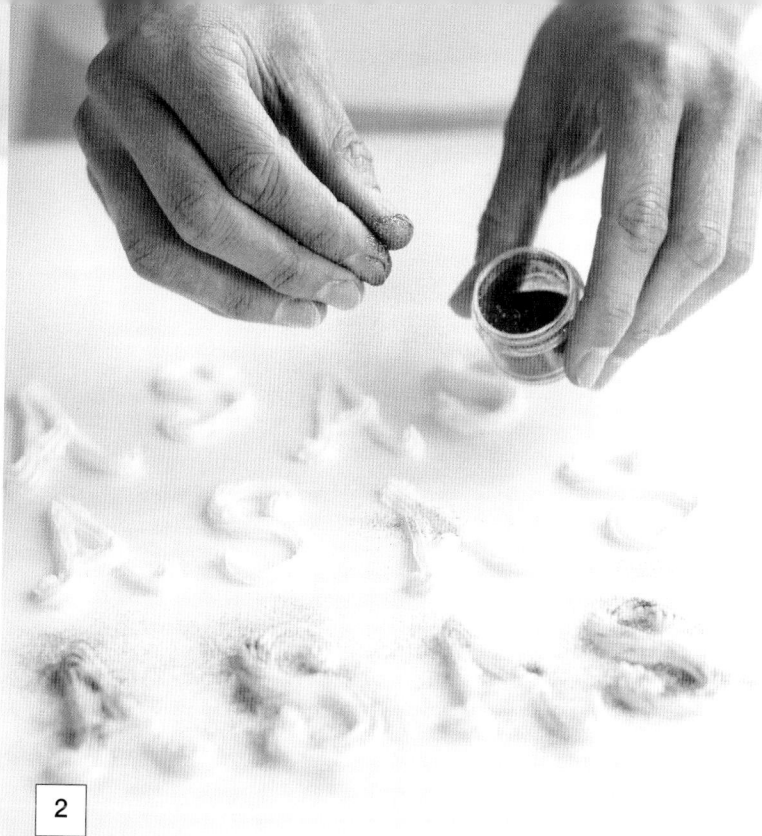

2

how to make
royal-icing letters

✳ Fill the piping bag with the small star-shaped nozzle with the Royal Icing.

✳ Put the baking tray lined with baking parchment in front of you on the work surface.

✳ Pipe the required letters onto the baking parchment. Take it slowly until you get used to making the letters and make sure that separate strokes within a letter are well attached so that they don't break off when you stand them up later. **(1)**

✳ While the icing is still wet, sprinkle with edible glitter. **(2)**

✳ Make more letters than you require to allow for breakages.

✳ Set aside to dry for at least 48 hours.

I found these mini terracotta pots in my garden centre and they are the perfect scale to serve these cupcakes in, but you can leave them out of the recipe if you can't find them. Piping flowers in buttercream is really quite simple, but practice makes perfect. If at first you're not happy with your flowers, simply scrape the buttercream off the top of the cakes and start again. You can buy nozzles especially for making petals – they are curved and usually called petal or leaf nozzles – but do experiment with different shapes to find the most effective ones.

little flower pots

1 quantity Buttermilk Sponge (page 9)

1 quantity Meringue Buttercream (page 11)

assorted food colouring pastes

tiny sugar flowers

muffin tin, lined with 8–10 paper cupcake cases

mini-muffin tin, lined with 8–10 paper cases in the coordinating size

mini terracotta pots in 2 sizes

piping bags fitted with assorted petal nozzles (see page 14 for some of the nozzle shapes available)

makes about 16

Preheat the oven to 180°C (350°F) Gas 4.

Divide the Buttermilk Sponge mixture between the cupcake cases, filling them two-thirds full, and bake on the middle shelf of the preheated oven for 12–25 minutes. The time will vary according to the size of the cakes – keep an eye on them and take them out when they are well risen and a skewer inserted into the middle of the cakes comes out clean. Leave to cool in the tins for 5 minutes before transferring to a wire rack to cool completely.

Divide the Meringue Buttercream between however many bowls you need for the colours you're using and tint each one a different colour (see page 16 for help on tinting) using the food colouring pastes. Tint them the shade you like by very gradually adding more colouring.

Cover the top of each cold cupcake with buttercream, spreading evenly with a palette knife. Fit the piping bag with your chosen nozzle and fill with buttercream. Holding the bag at a 45-degree angle to the cake, pipe petal shapes over the top of the cakes. Finish off each cake with a tiny sugar flower in the centre.

Carefully place one cake in each terracotta pot to serve.

1 quantity Double Choc Sponge
or Buttermilk Sponge (page 9)

1 quantity Marshmallow
Frosting (page 11)

1 quantity Chocolate Glaze
(page 12)

hundreds and thousands

*1–2 muffin tins, lined with paper
cupcake cases*

*large piping bag with a plain
1-cm nozzle*

makes 12–16

**A rich, dark chocolate cupcake topped with a mound of luscious
marshmallowy frosting and coated in a glossy dark chocolate glaze.
Does a cupcake get any better than this?**

hi-hat cupcakes

Preheat the oven to 180°C (350°F) Gas 4.

Divide the Double Choc or Buttermilk Sponge mixture between the paper cupcake
cases, filling them two-thirds full, and bake on the middle shelf of the preheated
oven for 20 minutes, or until well risen and a skewer inserted into the middle of the
cupcakes comes out clean. Leave to cool in the tins for 5 minutes before transferring
to a wire rack to cool completely.

See opposite for instructions on how to decorate the cupcakes.

how to decorate

hi-hat cupcakes

✳ Fill the piping bag with the Marshmallow Frosting.

✳ Pipe the frosting into a cone shape on top of each cold cupcake. Don't pipe the frosting right to the edge of the cupcake – leave a border of about ½ cm between the frosting and the top of the paper case. **(1)**

✳ Leave the frosting to set for at least 30 minutes before coating in the Chocolate Glaze.

✳ When you've made the Chocolate Glaze, leave it to cool slightly before using. Make sure it's in a small but deep bowl, so that when you dip the cupcake hats in, they fit in without getting squashed.

✳ Holding the cupcake upside down, submerge the frosting in the glaze. Allow any excess glaze to drip back into the bowl. The frosting should be completely covered in chocolate glaze. **(2)**

✳ Leave to set for 5 minutes.

✳ Finally, scatter the hundreds and thousands over the top and leave until completely set.

These brownies are strictly for adults! They are rich, dark, sticky, very chocolatey and loaded with dried cherries and hazelnuts. They are just as good served plain without the frosting and with a scoop of luxury vanilla or chocolate ice cream. Make the chocolate and glass hearts in advance and store in a cool, dry place until ready to serve.

double chocolate, hazelnut and dried cherry brownie squares

150 g skinned hazelnuts

225 g dark chocolate, chopped

150 g unsalted butter

300 g light brown soft sugar or light muscovado

4 eggs

1 teaspoon vanilla extract

125 g plain flour

a pinch of salt

125 g dried cherries

to decorate

½ quantity Chocolate Fudge Frosting (page 12)

1 bag fruit-flavoured boiled sweets

150 g dark chocolate, chopped

pink and/or red sprinkles

23-cm square baking tin, greased and base-lined with baking parchment

assorted heart-shaped cutters, oiled

2 solid baking trays, lined with baking parchment

makes about 16

Preheat the oven to 180°C (350°F) Gas 4.

Put the hazelnuts on a baking tray and toast in the preheated oven for 5 minutes. Leave to cool slightly, then roughly chop and set aside. Leave the oven on.

Put the chocolate and butter in a heatproof bowl set over a pan of barely simmering water. Stir until smooth and thoroughly combined. Leave to cool slightly.

Put the eggs and sugar in the bowl of a freestanding electric mixer fitted with the whisk attachment (or use an electric whisk and mixing bowl) and beat until pale and light. Add the vanilla and chocolate mixture and mix until combined. Sift the flour and salt and fold into the mixture with the chopped hazelnuts and cherries.

Pour the mixture into the prepared baking tin and bake on the middle shelf of the hot oven for 25 minutes. Leave to cool in the tin until completely cold.

Spread the Chocolate Fudge Frosting over the cold brownie and leave to set before cutting into squares. Now see overleaf for instructions on how to make the hearts.

Arrange the 'glass' and speckled chocolate hearts on top of the brownie squares just before serving, as they can melt if left sitting in the frosting for too long.

1

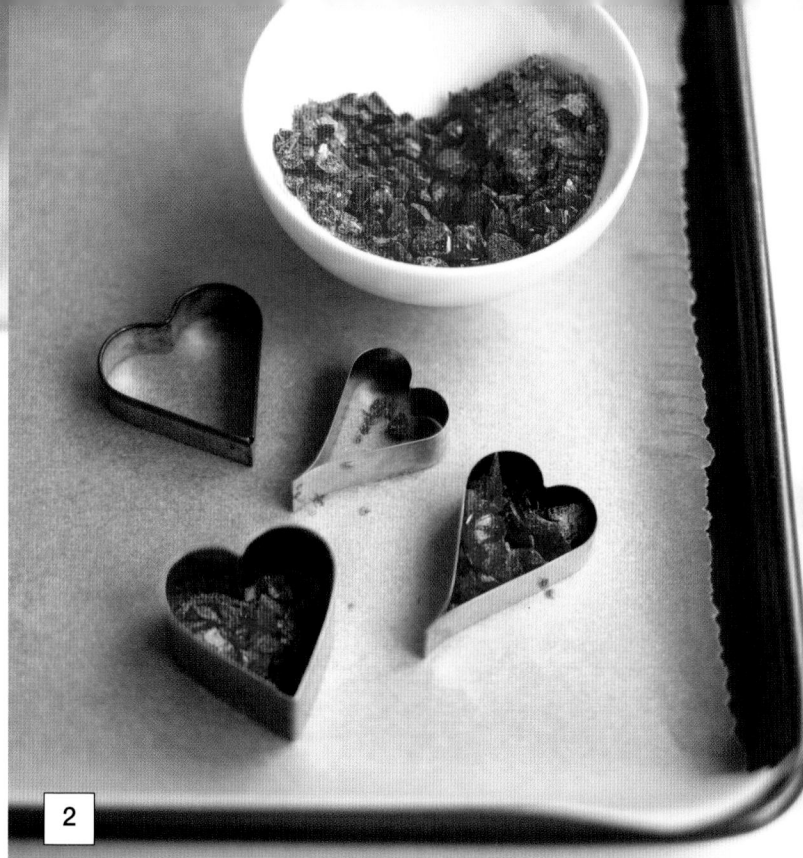

2

how to make
'glass' hearts

✳ Divide the boiled sweets into separate colours and pop into plastic food bags. Just use red ones for these hearts, if you like. Using a rolling pin or pestle and mortar, crush the sweets into small pieces. **(1)**

✳ Preheat the oven to 170°C (325°F) Gas 3, if possible on the conventional setting, not using the fan.

✳ Arrange the well-oiled heart-shaped cutters on one of the prepared baking trays. Make the hearts in small quantities, as you will need to work quickly once they come out of the oven.

✳ Carefully fill the cutters with the crushed sweets in an even, thin layer. **(2)**

✳ Bake on the middle shelf of the preheated oven for about 5 minutes, or until melted and smooth. You will need to keep a close eye on the timing, as it can vary depending on the size of cutters and the quantity of sweets used.

✳ Once the sweets have melted and filled the cutters, remove from the oven and leave to cool and harden for a couple of minutes. Very carefully push the 'glass' hearts from the cutters.

✳ Repeat with different colours as desired.

✳ The 'glass' hearts will keep for 24 hours in a cool, dry place.

how to make
speckled chocolate hearts

✳ Put the chocolate in a heatproof bowl set over a pan of barely simmering water. Stir until smooth and melted.

✳ Pour the melted chocolate onto the second prepared baking tray. Spread into a thin layer using a palette knife and set aside to cool for 5 minutes. **(3)**

✳ Scatter with pink and/or red sprinkles and leave until completely set and firm. **(4)**

✳ Using a heart-shaped cutter, carefully stamp out shapes from the chocolate. **(5)** Store either in a cool place or in the fridge until required.

5

Make the cake base the day before you plan to ice these cakes – this makes the fondant fancies easier to cut and ice. These little cakes are enough for just a couple of mouthfuls and look beautiful iced in contrasting delicate colours.

fondant fancies

150 g unsalted butter, softened

150 g caster sugar

2 eggs, beaten

150 g plain flour

2 teaspoons baking powder

3–4 tablespoons milk, at room temperature

50 g ground almonds

finely grated zest and freshly squeezed juice of ½ unwaxed lemon

2 tablespoons lemon curd

to decorate

1 tablespoon sieved apricot jam, warmed

icing sugar, for dusting

100 g natural marzipan

500-g pack fondant icing sugar

freshly squeezed juice of 1 lemon

pink food colouring paste

yellow food colouring paste

blue food colouring paste

150 g royal icing sugar

tiny sugar flowers

20-cm square baking tin, greased and base-lined with baking parchment

small piping bag with a fine writing nozzle, or make your own (see page 15)

makes 12—16

The day before you want to serve the fondant fancies, preheat the oven to 180°C (350°F) Gas 4.

Cream together the butter and sugar until light and creamy in the bowl of a freestanding mixer (or use an electric whisk and mixing bowl). Gradually add the beaten eggs, mixing well between each addition and scraping down the side of the mixing bowl from time to time.

Sift together the flour and baking powder and add to the mixture in alternate batches with the milk. Fold in the ground almonds, lemon zest and juice and stir until smooth.

Spoon the batter into the prepared baking tin. Spread level and bake on the middle shelf of the preheated oven for about 25 minutes, or until a skewer inserted into the middle of the cake comes out clean. Remove from the oven and leave to cool in the tin for 5–10 minutes before turning out onto a wire rack to cool completely.

The next day, split the cake in half horizontally using a long, serrated knife. Spread the lemon curd over the bottom layer and sandwich the 2 layers back together. Brush the warmed apricot jam over the top of the cake. Lightly dust a work surface with icing sugar. Roll out the marzipan to a square the same size as the top of the cake, using the baking tin as a guide. Lay the marzipan on top of the jam and smooth the surface. Trim the sides of the cake and then cut into neat, 4-cm cubes.

Mix the fondant icing sugar with enough lemon juice to make a smooth, thick icing suitable to coat the cakes. Divide the icing between 3 bowls and tint each one pink, yellow or blue (see page 16 for help on tinting) using the food colouring pastes. Tint them the shade you like by very gradually adding more colouring. Cover 2 of the bowls with clingfilm while you work with the third. Coat the top and sides of each cake with this colour of icing. The easiest way to do this is to hold one cake on a fork over the bowl and drizzle the icing over the top and sides to coat evenly. Transfer the cakes to a wire rack and leave for at least 1 hour, or until set. Continue with the other colours of icing until you have coated all the cakes.

Whisk together the royal icing sugar and a little water until it is thick enough to pipe. Spoon into the piping bag and use to pipe thin lines and dots over the top of each cake. Decorate with tiny sugar flowers. Leave to set before serving.

large cakes

This is the perfect cake for a celebration such as a wedding or christening. It's dark, dense and very rich. It would be delicious to serve as a dessert with a compote of summer berries and lightly whipped double cream. As the cake is very moist, it can be made a couple of days before icing and serving. It can also be frozen uniced, wrapped well in clingfilm. Defrost completely before icing.

rich chocolate celebration cake

300 g dark chocolate (at least 70% cocoa solids), chopped

200 g unsalted butter

6 eggs, separated

200 g caster sugar

150 g ground almonds

½ teaspoon cream of tartar

a pinch of salt

frosting

4 rounded tablespoons sieved apricot jam, warmed

icing sugar, for dusting

250 g natural marzipan

1 quantity Chocolate Ganache (page 12)

roses

350 g white sugar paste

pink food colouring paste

23-cm springform cake tin, greased, lightly floured and base-lined with baking parchment

serves 12—16

Preheat the oven to 180°C (350°F) Gas 4.

Put the chocolate and butter in a heatproof bowl set over a pan of barely simmering water. Stir until smooth and thoroughly combined. Leave to cool slightly.

Put the egg yolks and sugar in the bowl of a freestanding mixer fitted with the whisk attachment (or use an electric whisk and mixing bowl) and beat until pale and very thick. Stir in the chocolate mixture. Add the ground almonds and mix well.

Put the egg whites, cream of tartar and salt in a grease-free bowl and whisk until they just form stiff peaks. Fold a large spoonful of the egg whites into the chocolate mixture to loosen, then carefully fold in the remainder.

Spoon the mixture into the prepared cake tin and bake on the middle shelf of the preheated oven for about 1 hour, or until the cake has formed a crust and a skewer inserted into the middle of the cake comes out with a moist crumb. Remove from the oven and leave to cool in the tin.

Once the cake is completely cold (or the next day), it can be iced.

Place the cake on a wire rack set over a baking tray. If the top of the cake is uneven, you may need to slice it off to make a flat surface. Brush the top and side of the cake with some of the warmed apricot jam. Lightly dust a clean, dry work surface with icing sugar and roll the marzipan out into a large, thin round big enough to cover the whole cake. Lay the marzipan on top of the jam and smooth the surface. Trim the excess, then brush with a little more apricot jam.

Pour the slightly cooled and thickened Chocolate Ganache over the top of the cake and use a palette knife to smooth the top and side. Leave the cake in a cool place to allow the ganache to set.

Now see overleaf for instructions on how to make the roses.

Arrange the dried sugar-paste roses on the cake.

how to make
sugar-paste roses

❉ Tint the sugar paste different shades of pink (see page 16 for help on tinting) using the pink food colouring paste, very gradually adding more colouring for a stronger colour.

❉ Lay a large sheet of clingfilm on the work surface. Break off small nuggets of the sugar paste and roll between your hands to make little balls of different sizes. Place on the clingfilm.

❉ Cover with more clingfilm. Using your thumb, flatten each ball until quite thin. It doesn't matter if they're irregular discs. **(1)**

❉ Peel off the top layer of clingfilm. Start with a small disc of sugar paste and, using your fingers, gently roll the disc into a spiral to form the centre of the rose. **(2)**

❉ Take another petal and carefully wrap this around the central one, covering the seam. **(3)**

❉ As you add the petals, gently squeeze the edges to make them more shapely and curved. Continue until you have created a rose in the size you require. **(4)**

❉ Pinch off any excess sugar paste from under the rose and stand it upright on baking parchment. Continue until you have the required number of roses, then leave them to dry for 2 days.

I like to serve this pretty cake for Mother's Day or when I have a girly gathering. Choose rose petals in two different shapes of pink and crystallize them as described on page 66. The cake can be baked and the fresh coconut shavings toasted a day in advance.

pistachio, coconut and lime cake

175 g shelled, unsalted pistachio nuts

75 g desiccated coconut

finely grated zest of 2 limes and freshly squeezed juice of 1

125 g plain flour

2 teaspoons baking powder

a pinch of salt

225 g unsalted butter, softened

225 g caster sugar

4 eggs, beaten

1 teaspoon rosewater

to decorate

½ fresh coconut

finely grated zest and freshly squeezed juice of 2 limes

200–250 g icing sugar, sifted

50 g shelled pistachio nuts, chopped

pink rose petals, crystallized (page 66)

23-cm ring cake tin, greased and lightly floured

baking tray, lined with baking parchment

serves 6—8

Preheat the oven to 180°C (350°F) Gas 4.

Put the pistachio nuts in a food processor and pulse until finely chopped. Mix with the desiccated coconut and lime zest. In a separate bowl, sift together the flour, baking powder and salt.

Cream together the butter and sugar until light and creamy in the bowl of a freestanding mixer (or use an electric whisk and mixing bowl). Gradually add the beaten eggs, mixing well between each addition and scraping down the side of the mixing bowl from time to time. Add the rosewater and mix again.

Add the pistachio nuts, coconut and lime zest and mix until smooth. Add the sifted dry ingredients and mix again. Finally, add the lime juice and beat until smooth.

Pour the mixture into the prepared cake tin, spread level and bake on the middle shelf of the preheated oven for about 35–40 minutes, or until a skewer inserted into the middle of the cake comes out clean. Leave to cool in the tin for 5 minutes, then carefully turn out onto a wire rack to cool completely. Leave the oven on.

To decorate, crack open the coconut and remove the flesh. Using a vegetable peeler, shave the flesh into strips. Arrange the strips in a single layer on the prepared baking tray and toast in the hot oven for about 10 minutes, or until lightly golden. Keep an eye on it, as it can easily burn.

Put the lime zest, juice and icing sugar in a bowl and beat until smooth and the right consistency to just drip over the edges of the cake. You may need a little more or less icing sugar depending on how juicy the limes are.

Place the cake on a serving plate and, using a spoon, carefully cover the top of the cake with the icing, allowing some to dip over the sides. Leave to set.

Scatter the cooled, toasted coconut shavings, chopped pistachio nuts and crystallized rose petals all over the iced cake and serve.

I have decorated this cake with small sugar-paste flowers. These are so easy to make – just follow the instructions on page 125 (and leave to dry out for 2 days) or look out for ready-made ones in sugarcraft shops. If you prefer, you could always decorate your teapot with a selection of sweets. For the teapot, you'll need to make the recipe below twice so that you have 2 identical cake pieces for the finished pot.

tea for two

for half of the teapot

175 g unsalted butter, softened

175 g caster sugar

3 eggs, beaten

1 teaspoon vanilla extract

175 g plain flour

3 teaspoons baking powder

3 tablespoons milk, at room temperature

to decorate

icing sugar, for dusting

150 g white sugar paste

lilac food colouring paste

blue colouring paste

1 quantity Marshmallow Frosting (page 11)

4 tablespoons sieved apricot jam, warmed

a little Royal Icing (page 13) (optional)

yellow food colouring paste (optional)

3 sticks of dowelling

assorted small flower-shaped cutters

small piping bag with a fine writing nozzle, or make your own (see page 15)

1-litre ovenproof Pyrex bowl, greased and lightly floured

serves 8

Make the teapot handle and spout at least 2 days before you make the cake. Lightly dust a clean, dry work surface with icing sugar. Take 40 g of the sugar paste and roll to make a sausage shape with one end slightly thicker than the other. Bend into a spout shape. Take another 40 g of the sugar paste and roll to make a sausage shape. Bend into a handle shape. Push a length of dowelling into both ends of the handle and the thicker end of the spout so that they stick out by at least 4 cm.

Turn to page 125 to make sugar-paste flowers with the remaining sugar paste. At the same time, make a small ball to go on top of the teapot lid. Leave both the flowers, teapot handle and spout to dry out completely on baking parchment for at least 2 days before using.

When you are ready to make the cake, preheat the oven to 180°C (350°F) Gas 4 and position the shelf in the bottom third of the oven.

Cream together the butter and sugar until light and creamy in the bowl of a freestanding mixer (or use an electric whisk and mixing bowl). Gradually add the beaten eggs, mixing well between each addition and scraping down the side of the mixing bowl from time to time. Add the vanilla.

Sift together the flour and baking powder. Add to the cake mixture along with the milk and mix until smooth.

Spoon the mixture into the prepared Pyrex bowl and spread level with a palette knife. Bake in the preheated oven for about 45 minutes, or until a skewer inserted in the middle of the cake comes out clean. Leave to cool in the bowl for 5 minutes before turning out onto a wire rack to cool completely.

Repeat as above for the second half of the teapot.

Now refer to the step instructions overleaf for assembling the cake.

1

2

how to assemble
a teapot cake

✳ Place one cake, rounded side down, on a serving plate. Using a palette knife, cover the flat side with Marshmallow Frosting. **(1)**

✳ Lay the second cake, rounded side up, on top of this cake. Brush the apricot jam all over the cake. Cover the whole cake with marshmallow frosting, spreading smoothly with a palette knife. **(2)**

✳ Get the spout, handle and sugar-paste flowers ready. **(3)**

✳ Before the frosting sets, arrange the flowers over the teapot, pressing them onto the frosting. Top with the ball for the lid. **(4)**

✳ Push the handle and spout into either side of the cake, allowing the bottom of the handle to rest on the serving plate.

✳ If you like, you can finish off the flowers with a dot of yellow-tinted royal icing in the centres.

3

To get ahead, make the cake base and the cookie dough for this fabulous creation the day before you plan to serve it.

dog kennel

250 g unsalted butter, softened

250 g caster sugar

4 eggs, beaten

1 teaspoon vanilla extract

250 g plain flour

4 teaspoons baking powder

3–4 tablespoons milk, at room temperature

1 quantity Vanilla Buttercream (page 12)

200 g milk chocolate, for the chocolate panels

25 g white chocolate

200–250 g milk chocolate buttons

50 g white chocolate chips

dogs

1 quantity Gingerbread Biscuits (page 10)

plain flour, for dusting

1 quantity Royal Icing (page 13)

assorted food colouring pastes, to match your breeds of dog!

23 x 33 x 6-cm baking tin, lined with baking parchment and greased

assorted dog-shaped cookie cutters

2 baking trays, lined with baking parchment

small piping bag with a fine writing nozzle, or make your own (see page 15)

serves 8—10

Preheat the oven to 180°C (350°F) Gas 4.

Cream together the butter and sugar until light and creamy. Gradually add the beaten eggs, mixing well between each addition and scraping down the side of the mixing bowl from time to time. Add the vanilla. Sift together the flour and baking powder and add to the mixture in 2 batches. Stir in the milk. Mix until smooth, then spoon into the prepared baking tin and spread level with a palette knife. Bake on the middle shelf of the preheated oven for 35–40 minutes, or until a skewer inserted into the middle of the cake comes out clean. Leave to cool in the tin for 5 minutes before turning out onto a wire rack to cool completely. Once cold, wrap in clingfilm until you are ready to assemble the dog kennel. Leave the oven on to bake the dog biscuits.

Take the Gingerbread Biscuit dough out of the fridge and put it on a lightly floured work surface. Roll it out to a thickness of 3–4 mm. Using the cookie cutters, carefully stamp out dog shapes. Arrange them on the prepared baking trays. Gather together the off-cuts of the dough and re-roll to make more shapes. Bake the biscuits on the middle shelf of the preheated oven for 10–12 minutes, or until firm and the edges are just starting to brown, swapping the trays over if needed. Leave to cool on the trays for about 5 minutes before transferring to a wire rack to cool completely.

Divide the Royal Icing between however many bowls you need for the colours you're using and tint each one a different colour (see page 16 for help on tinting) using the food colouring pastes. Fill the piping bag with whichever colour you want to start with. Pipe borders around the cold biscuits. 'Flood' the area inside the borders with icing (see page 44 for step pictures of 'flooding'), spreading it carefully up to the edges with a mini palette knife or small knife. Leave it to dry and harden slightly, then decorate or accessorize as you like!

When you are ready to assemble the cake, cut it into quarters and place one quarter on a serving platter. Cover the top with 2 tablespoons of the Vanilla Buttercream, spreading evenly with a palette knife. Repeat so that you have 4 layers of cake and 3 layers of buttercream. Using a long, sharp knife, cut into the long sides to make a roof shape. Cover the whole cake with buttercream and leave somewhere cool.

Make the chocolate panels as described on page 121. At the same time, make a door shape out of the white chocolate. Cut the panels to fit the walls of the dog kennel (vertically for the short sides and horizontally for the long). Stick them to the buttercream. Attach the door with a little buttercream. Tile the roof with the chocolate buttons and chips. Arrange the dogs in front of the kennel and serve.

This is really a grown-up Victoria Sponge with a few mouth-watering added extras. The meringue buttercream gets an extra hit of vanilla with the addition of the seeds from a vanilla pod. Try to use small, extra-sweet berries – fraises des bois are particularly pretty – and the best possible strawberry jam you can find. If you were to use home-made jam, that would take this cake all the way to the top.

high summer cake

225 g unsalted butter, softened

300 g caster sugar

4 eggs, beaten

2 teaspoons vanilla extract

finely grated zest of 1 unwaxed lemon

375 g plain flour

2 teaspoons baking powder

1 teaspoon bicarbonate of soda

a pinch of salt

200 ml buttermilk

6 tablespoons strawberry jam

1 quantity Meringue Buttercream (page 11, but using seeds scraped out of a vanilla pod in place of the vanilla extract)

200 g white chocolate, coarsely grated

350 g small strawberries and/or fraises des bois (if possible)

250 g raspberries

125 g redcurrants, crystallized (page 66)

2 x 20-cm round cake tins, greased and base-lined with baking parchment

serves 8

Preheat the oven to 180°C (350°F) Gas 4.

Cream together the butter and sugar until light and creamy in the bowl of a freestanding mixer (or use an electric whisk and mixing bowl). Gradually add the beaten eggs, mixing well between each addition and scraping down the side of the mixing bowl from time to time. Add the vanilla and lemon zest and mix again.

Sift together the flour, baking powder, bicarbonate of soda and salt. Add to the cake mixture with the buttermilk and mix again until smooth.

Divide the mixture between the prepared cake tins and bake on the middle shelf of the preheated oven for about 35 minutes, or until well risen, golden and a skewer inserted into the middle of the cakes comes out clean. Leave to cool in the tins for 5 minutes, then transfer to a wire rack to cool completely.

Cut the cold cakes in half horizontally, using a long, serrated knife. Place one layer on a serving plate and spread with 2 tablespoons of the strawberry jam. Spread 2 tablespoons of the Meringue Buttercream over the jam and top with another cake layer. Repeat with the remaining cake layers, leaving the top layer plain. Gently press the cake layers together. Cover the side of the cake with buttercream, spreading evenly with a palette knife.

Scatter the grated white chocolate onto a tray and, holding the cake very carefully in both hands, roll the side in the grated chocolate to coat completely. Spread a thick layer of buttercream on top of the cake and finish with the mixed berries and crystallized redcurrants. Serve immediately.

This cake looks wildly impressive, but is actually quite easy to make and assemble. You just need to allow plenty of time and patience – it's not one to be knocked up in an afternoon. Make the cake layers the day before you plan to serve the finished cake.

dark and white chocolate layer cake

125 g dark chocolate, chopped

300 g plain flour

2 teaspoons bicarbonate of soda

a pinch of salt

125 g unsalted butter, softened

400 g light brown soft sugar

4 eggs, beaten

1 teaspoon vanilla extract

225 ml soured cream

225 ml boiling water

1 quantity Chocolate Meringue Buttercream (page 11)

ganache

225 ml double cream

25 g unsalted butter

25 g caster sugar

200 g dark chocolate, finely chopped

1 teaspoon coffee essence (preferably Camp)

chocolate panels

200 g dark chocolate, chopped

200 g white chocolate, chopped

2 x 20-cm square cake tins, greased, base-lined with baking parchment and greased

2 piping bags with star-shaped nozzles

baking tray, lined with baking parchment

serves 16

Preheat the oven to 180°C (350°F) Gas 4.

Put the chocolate for the cake in a heatproof bowl set over a pan of barely simmering water. Stir until smooth and melted. Leave to cool slightly.

Sift the flour, bicarbonate of soda and salt into a bowl.

Cream together the butter and sugar until light and creamy. Gradually add the beaten eggs, mixing well between each addition and scraping down the side of the mixing bowl from time to time. Add the vanilla and melted chocolate and mix. Mix in one-third of the sifted dry ingredients, followed by half the soured cream. Repeat and finish with the remaining third of the sifted dry ingredients. Now add the boiling water, mixing well to ensure everything is thoroughly combined.

Divide the mixture between the prepared cake tins, spread level and bake on the middle shelf of the preheated oven for about 30–35 minutes, or until a skewer inserted into the middle of the cakes comes out clean. Leave to cool in the tins for 5–10 minutes, then turn out onto a wire rack to cool completely. If you are not assembling the cakes straightaway, wrap in clingfilm until needed.

To make the ganache, put the cream, butter and sugar in a small saucepan and heat until just boiling. Pour over the chopped chocolate and leave to melt for 5 minutes. Add the coffee essence, stir to combine, then set aside.

When you are ready to assemble the cake, cut the cold cakes in half horizontally, using a long, serrated knife. Place one layer on a serving plate and spread with 3–4 tablespoons of the Chocolate Meringue Buttercream. Top with a second cake layer and spread with 3–4 tablespoons of ganache. Top with a third cake layer and spread with more buttercream. Top with the last cake layer. Gently press the layers together. Now spread buttercream evenly all over the top and side of the cake.

Fill one piping bag with the remaining buttercream and the other with the remaining ganache. Pipe rosettes in straight lines across the top of the cake, alternating between buttercream and ganache.

Now see opposite for instructions on how to make the chocolate panels.

Arrange the dark and white chocolate panels alternately around the outside of the cake, pressing them into the buttercream to stick.

1

2

how to make
chocolate panels

✳ Put the dark chocolate in a heatproof bowl set over a pan of barely simmering water. Stir until thoroughly smooth and melted.

✳ Pour the melted chocolate onto the prepared baking tray. Spread into a thin layer using a palette knife and set aside until completely set.

✳ Using a large, sharp knife, trim the edges of the chocolate to make an even rectangle. Cut into strips about 2 cm wide. **(1)**

✳ Trim the strips so that they are just a little taller than the frosted cake. **(2)**

✳ Repeat the steps above with the white chocolate.

I have made the flowers on this cake in a variety of colours to match the feather butterflies hovering above the cake. Look out for feather butterflies and ribbons in good haberdashers. Make the beautiful sugar-paste flowers 2 days in advance to allow them time to dry out.

blossom cake

1 quantity Buttermilk Sponge (page 9)

6 tablespoons lemon curd

3 tablespoons mascarpone

3 tablespoons sieved apricot jam, warmed

to decorate

250 g white sugar paste

yellow food colouring paste

orange food colouring paste

pink food colouring paste

red food colouring paste

500 g natural marzipan

500 g white ready-to-roll fondant icing

2–3 tablespoons icing sugar, plus extra for dusting

assorted small flower-shaped cutters

embossing tools (optional)

2 x 20-cm round cake tins, greased, base-lined with baking parchment and greased

small piping bag with a fine writing nozzle, or make your own (see page 15)

feather butterflies (optional)

white craft wire

wide ribbon to match your colour scheme

serves 8

See overleaf for step instructions on how to make sugar-paste flowers. Leave to dry out for 2 days before you make the cake.

When you are ready to make the cake, preheat the oven to 180°C (350°F) Gas 4.

Divide the Buttermilk Sponge mixture between the prepared cake tins, spread level and bake on the middle shelf of the preheated oven for about 25 minutes, or until a skewer inserted into the middle of the cakes comes out clean. You may need to turn the tins halfway through cooking. Leave to cool in the tins for 5 minutes before turning out onto a wire rack to cool completely.

Cut the cold cakes in half horizontally, using a long, serrated knife. Place one layer on a serving plate and spread with half the lemon curd. Cover with another cake layer and spread this with the mascarpone. Top with a third cake layer and spread with the remaining lemon curd. Top with the last cake layer. Gently press the layers together. Brush the warmed apricot jam all over the cake.

Lightly dust a work surface with icing sugar. Roll out the marzipan to a thickness of 3 mm. Using a rolling pin, carefully transfer the marzipan to the cake and drape it on top to cover completely. Using your hands, smooth the marzipan over the top and side and trim off any excess. Brush the marzipan with a little boiled water.

Roll out the fondant icing and cover the cake with it in the same way as you did with the marzipan. Set aside to dry for a couple of hours.

In a small bowl, mix the icing sugar with a tiny amount of water to make a paste. Fill the piping bag with this icing and pipe small dots on the underside of each sugar-paste flower. Stick them around the side and on top of the cake. Stick the tiny sugar-paste balls to the centres of the flowers with a dot of icing.

Attach the feather butterflies to wires, if using, and push into the cake so that they hover delicately above the blossoms. Finally, wrap a coordinating ribbon around the bottom of the cake and secure with a small dot of icing.

how to make
sugar-paste flowers

✳ Tint the sugar paste yellow, orange, pink and red (see page 16 for help on tinting) using the food colouring pastes. Tint them the shades you like by very gradually adding more colouring.

✳ Lightly dust a clean, dry work surface with icing sugar. Roll the sugar paste out to a thickness of 2–3 mm. Chop off tiny pieces and roll into balls for the centres of the flowers.

✳ Using the assorted flower-shaped cutters, stamp out flowers in a variety of shapes and sizes. Create details on the flowers with embossing tools or a wooden skewer.

✳ Press the flowers over the backs of spoons to create more interesting shapes while they set. Leave them to dry for 2 days.

suppliers and stockists

The Bakers Boutique
www.thebakersboutique.com
Tel: 020 8333 1559
Supplier of beautiful laser-cut cupcake and cake wrappers. Order online (in bulk) or check distributors page for details of your nearest stockist.

Blue Ribbons
www.blueribbons.co.uk
Tel: 020 8941 1591
Shop and online supplier of a wide range of cake decorating supplies, including seasonal items.

Cakes Cookies & Crafts Shop
www.cakescookiesandcraftsshop.co.uk
Tel: 01524 389 684
Wide selection of bakeware, cutters and cake decorations, plus an extensive range of Wilton piping bag nozzles in all sorts of shapes and sizes. Also, lustres, sugar strands, nonpareils, sprinkles, glitter and sugar flowers.

The Cook's Kitchen
http://thecookskitchen.com
Tel: 0844 3574772
Suppliers of quality cake tins and bakeware, plus decorating tools such as cake stencils, decorative cupcake wrappers and embossing tools.

Design a Cake
www.design-a-cake.co.uk
Tel: 0191 417 1572
Shop and online supplier with a large selection of sugarcraft and baking items including stencils.

H. O. Foose Tinsmithing
www.foosecookiecutters.com
US-based supplier with an incredible selection of more than 700 hand-made cookie cutters. If you can't find what you're looking for on this site you can buy kits to make up your own designs. They also do lots of miniature cutters which are useful for sugar paste and fondant icing shapes. They ship to the UK but allow plenty of time for delivery from USA.

Jane Asher
www.jane-asher.co.uk
22–24 Cale Street
London SW3 3QU
Tel: 020 7584 6177
Shop and online supplier of a wide range of cake baking and decorating supplies, including tiny cutters and embossing tools.

John Lewis
www.johnlewis.com
Tel: 08456 049 049
A lovely range of bakeware, from vintage-style mixing bowls and measuring cups to seasonal and shaped cupcake cases and pretty cookie cutters.

Lakeland
www.lakeland.co.uk
Tel: 01539 488 100
See online for details of your nearest store. Huge selection of kitchen and baking equipment, such as cupcake tins, cake decorations, storage containers, etc. as well as a stand designed especially to display cupcakes. Plus a selection of flower-shaped cutters in a range of sizes.

Lindy's Cakes
www.lindyscakes.co.uk
Tel: 01296 622 418
Selection of sugarcraft and cake baking items including embossing sticks.

Make a Wish!
www.makeawishcakeshop.co.uk
This is quite possibly one of the largest selections of cake decorating items available online that I have found. Sugar flowers, tiny cutters, pretty ribbons and much, much more.

Squires Kitchen
www.squires-shop.com
Tel: 0845 22 55 671
Large retailer of cake decorating and sugarcraft supplies with more than 4,000 products, for example, edible gold and silver leaf and assorted shoe-shaped cookie cutters!

Steamer Trading
www.mycookshop.com
Tel: 01273 403 000
Sussex cookshops and online supplier of quality cookware.

The publisher would like to thank **KitchenAid** for the loan of the stand mixer featured in this book. Visit **www.kitchenaid.com** for more of their products and your nearest stockist.

index

acknowledgements

I would like to thank the very lovely Kate Whitaker for her beautiful pictures in this book – she's a girl who really knows how to bring a penguin cupcake to life!

And a huge thank you to Penny Markham for her beautiful plates and tableware.

To Steve and Céline at Ryland Peters & Small for their patience, utter fabulousness and extraordinary hard work.

Also, thank you to our wonderful hand models, Céline, Amy and Mima for stepping in and holding piping bags when my hands were covered in frosting and food colouring!

And to my parents, M and R, an enormous thank you for yet again more dog-sitting, for just being there when I need you and for being so wonderful. Mungo says thanks too!